From Downsizing to Recovery

From Downsizing to Recovery

Strategic Transition Options for Organizations and Individuals

Richard L. Knowdell
Elizabeth Branstead
Milan Moravec

CPP Books
Palo Alto, California
A Division of Consulting Psychologists Press, Inc.

MBTI and *Myers-Briggs Type Indicator* are registered trademarks of Consulting Psychologists Press, Inc.

The *Strong Interest Inventory* refers to the *Strong Vocational Interest Blanks,* a registered trademark of Stanford University Press.

The following publishers have generously given permission to use extended quotations from copyrighted works: From *Operation ABLE 1990 – 91 Annual Report,* Chicago: Operation ABLE. From *OITC Tax Bulletin,* August 21, 1992, Washington, DC: Association of Outplacement Consulting Firms International. Used by permission of Mike Curran, NOVA PIC, Sunnyvale, CA.

Jacket design Mark Ong
Cover illustration © Geoff Golson/The Image Bank
Interior illustration Richard Sigberman

97 96 95 94   10 9 8 7 6 5 4 3 2 1

Printed in the United States of America

Library of Congress Cataloging-in-Publication Data
Knowdell, Richard L.
    From downsizing to recovery : strategic transition options
for organizations and individuals / Richard Knowdell,
Elizabeth Branstead, Milan Moravec. -- 1st ed.
      p.   cm.
    Includes bibliographical references and index.
    ISBN 0-89106-067-7
    1. Employees--Dismissal of--Planning. 2. Downsizing of
organizations. 3. Career changes. I. Branstead, Elizabeth.
II. Moravec, Milan.   III. Title.
HF5549.5.D55K58 1994
658.1'6--dc20
94-8909
CIP

First edition
    First printing 1994

This book is dedicated to those involved in the downsizing and outplacement processes: the senior executives who must make the difficult decision to downsize, the human resource management staff who are tasked with coordinating the downsizing, the frontline managers who face the difficult task of notifying valued employees (and often friends) that their jobs have been eliminated, the outplacement professionals who are brought in to assist the terminated employees in securing new jobs, the outplacement managers who must train the growing ranks of outplacement counselors, business school professors who must introduce the new and often little understood role of "terminator" to their management students, and, finally, the outplaced employees and their families who are struggling to get on with their lives.

Contents

Preface

Downsizing, whether we like it or not, is now part of organizational life, and the strategy of downsizing has become an accepted business practice. This book is a guide through the maze of organizational and individual pain and opportunity, legal issues, planning, and regeneration. There are three major focuses:

- It is a comprehensive, practical guide for downsizing written for managers, key decision makers, and implementors, as well as for those who provide career transition services for the organization and individuals.

- It is designed to address the human implication of downsizing—its effects on executives, managers, individuals, the community-at-large, and stakeholders.

- It is a book with forward movement. There is new life and a renewed opportunity to demonstrate leadership in reengineering the organization.

Until the decade of the 1990s, we dealt with downsizing and outplacement by the seat of our pants. The topic was virtually absent from management development programs and MBA curricula. For all too many managers, the first time they ever thought seriously about downsizing and layoffs was when their bosses told them that it was their job to notify members of their department that they were to be laid off—the next morning. We have now learned from our experiences and reached the time when it is possible to adequately prepare and plan for downsizings, the resulting workforce reduction, and, hopefully, the reengineering of the organization into a successful competitor.

The book is divided into three sections:

Section One: Managing the Downsizing Process.   In this section, we focus on end results, beginning with decisions that must be made before downsizing: What kind of changes does the enterprise really need? Can these desired changes be accomplished without reducing the workforce? What are the options that are available to managers? We include legal issues, COBRA benefits, and federal regulations. This is followed by a chapter on preparing management for downsizing: What are the roles of the board of directors? senior executives? other managers? What do they need to do to effectively handle downsizing? The last chapter in this section deals with the actual workforce reduction. Throughout this section we describe the pivotal role that human resource managers play and provide sample letters and checklists that make their contributions more effective.

Section Two: Providing for the Displaced Worker.   These three chapters focus on the services that can be provided to the exiting employee—either from within the organization or externally. There is an enormous range of options that will help the employee move from the downsized business and into a new organization and perhaps into a new career. While helping individuals to move onward is a noble and honorable action, it is also a direct means of helping managers and the ongoing strategic workforce transition to the future.

Section Three: The Bridge to the Future.   The central factor amid all this turbulence is the workforce. People provide the new ideas essential to business competitiveness as well as the skills, expertise, energy, and commitment to transform those ideas into reality. To keep the business healthy, a systems approach is necessary: Business values are aligned with individual values as well as with corporate culture, vision, and the expectations of customers, vendors, and other stakeholders.

The lessons learned here are that leading a downsizing is a complex process involving the entire enterprise and affecting a large and diverse population. The more comprehensive the process, the faster an organization can revitalize and the more quickly the workforce—which is the organization—can rethink and recommit to future business success.

The ideas we have used in this book have come from a rich diversity of hands-on and consulting experiences we have had in organization and individual career transformation. We draw from our experience in such sectors as engineering, research and development, global manufacturing and construction, high-tech research, higher education, government (local, state, and federal), energy-oil and utilities, healthcare systems, electronics, biotechnology/pharmaceuticals, transportation, financial services, international and domestic shipping, computer products, semiconductors, telecommunications, software, paper and wood products, entertainment, retail sales, and banking and finance.

The future is not something that just happens. It is something you create. You can "wing it" or make informed decisions about downsizing. Nobody has all the answers but somebody may have already learned what you need to know. Some have an opportunity for success and some are wise enough to grasp it. We have attempted to offer guidelines for moving from downsizing to recovery—and beyond.

SECTION ONE

MANAGING THE DOWNSIZING PROCESS

1

Disaster and Opportunity

Driving toward Streeter-Haaz's office complex, Stuart Aubret, President and CEO, noticed the sun shining on the nearby lake, but his mood remained dark. The agenda for the morning's meeting was to deal with a subject he had hoped to avoid. The company he had worked so hard to build was in serious trouble, buffeted by competition both domestic and, lately, international. These competitors were getting their products to the market more quickly and were taking increasingly bigger bites out of Streeter-Haaz's market share. Meanwhile, Streeter-Haaz's costs were rapidly escalating. It was time to confront the necessity for restructuring and streamlining the organization. How, Stuart wondered, could this be done without shattering the corporate culture? With complete sincerity, he had assured his organization that they were all "family." But now the specter of downsizing had stepped from the pages of *Time* and *Fortune* to appear on his doorstep, and both the company's future and its carefully nurtured climate of trust were in danger. Never in his administration had the need for careful strategy and planning been more urgent. As he approached corporate headquarters, he reflected on the events that had brought Streeter-Haaz to this precarious point.

Senior Vice President Carlos Portillo, his heir apparent, was on his way to the same meeting, feeling similar apprehension. If we can't avoid layoffs, I'm going to have to make some painful decisions, he thought. Can we keep that from happening? If not, how can I determine the right thing to do?

In the elevator, Carlos exchanged wan smiles with Christina Perugia, Senior Vice President of Human Resources, who was carrying a stack of data about employees, their positions, and their skills. The two would be working closely together, with Christina's department as coach, to implement the decisions made in this meeting. Neither said aloud the thought that was rising to the surface of both their minds: Is my own job safe?

Across town, Stephen Lee, a member of Streeter-Haaz's board of directors, was aware of the meeting and had already discussed with Stuart the necessity for carrying out restructuring in a way that was prudent for the business and in the best interests of the shareholders. He hoped that Stuart and his managers would plan their moves carefully, with due attention given to long-term issues.

ADMITTING THE GAME HAS CHANGED

With increasing frequency, similar scenarios are being played out worldwide in private-sector, public-sector, and nonprofit businesses of all sizes. As change has become the norm, workforce restructuring and downsizing have become part of organizational reality. No longer can a company promise (and keep that promise) that it will never let its employees go. IBM Corporation, the nation's longest running and best-known example of "employment for life," has evolved from a strict no-layoff policy through a series of voluntary early retirements to a situation of actually asking people to leave. In the mid-1980s, a high-flying computer chip maker bragged in its employment posters that, unlike its competition, it had a policy of never "using up its employees and discarding them like empty aluminum cans." But the aluminum can posters were quickly removed from the company's employment lobby on the day the firm announced its first layoff.

The downsizing epidemic is not limited to high-tech firms or to the United States. British Petroleum, Renault, Phillips, Barclays, Olivetti, Sabena World Airlines, and a host of other European firms have had to slash their staffs. Australia's Westpac Banking Corporation has been steadily downsized. In Japan, that bastion of lifetime employment, U.S.–owned firms have introduced the concept of layoffs. An executive of one of these companies commented, "They're ready for it." They may, in fact, have little choice.

As daily stories in the business press have been attesting for several years, no one's job is safe from the downsizing ax. Even competent, skilled employees, of whatever age, are vulnerable. Today's hottest technician or manager may well be handed a separation package tomorrow. Career transition firms, which help displaced workers with career changes, constitute one of very few growing industries, along with temporary agencies, designed to meet the needs of out-of-work staff and cautious companies. The proliferation of job support groups, career counseling organizations, and job fairs provides further proof that society recognizes the need for a career transition infrastructure to help ex-employees make the transition to new jobs.

A 1991 survey of the 4,500 largest companies in the United States, conducted by *Fortune* magazine and the Wyatt Company consulting firm, revealed that 86 percent of these organizations had downsized in the previous five years and most of them expected to have to do it again. A study by the American Management Association (AMA) lists five primary reasons for reducing the size of the workforce:

- Actual or anticipated downturn in business   55%
- Efforts to improve productivity   23%
- Mergers or acquisitions   9%
- Transfer of work   8%
- Automation or new technical processes   3%

For public-sector and nonprofit organizations, we might add another factor, especially acute in the continuing soft economy: reduced funding.

MAJOR SHIFTS IN THE BUSINESS CLIMATE

But as the economy improves and stabilizes, downsizing will become a thing of the past, right? Wrong. The expansiveness, both psychological and literal, of the early eighties is gone forever, or at least for the foreseeable future. The reasons given by the AMA survey respondents reflect the pressures of a fiercely dynamic global environment in which the cycles of "normal" business activity are growing shorter every year and even the concept of "normal" has become a moving target. Never before have so many rapid changes been taking place in five areas simultaneously (see Gyr, 1991).

Business environment.   With worldwide trade barriers falling, more companies, offshore and domestic, are going after the same share of the market. The outbreak of peace has dramatically altered priorities in both government and private-sector organizations. Companies in the United States are moving operations and information systems to new strategic locations, some halfway around the globe. As recessions hit different parts of the world, a company's business may be booming in Germany but suffering in Taiwan. Companies have to cope with new regulations (or deregulations) not only abroad but at home as well. Airlines and banking are just two examples of once-stable industries that used to enjoy the protection of strict regulation but now have to jockey for position among competitors, both old and new. Who knows? Some day air passengers may be able to conduct banking transactions as they travel. Airlines may even become banking institutions.

Structure.   Mergers, acquisitions, takeovers, and spinoffs are causing chaos in industry strategies. Organizations are disintegrating and reforming faster than Eastern European nations. In some large corporations, centralization and decentralization are taking place simultaneously. New strategic alliances are emerging; ten years ago, who would have thought that archcompetitors IBM and Apple would join forces?

Technology.   Technological advances are obviating the need for entire classes of employees. On the other hand, technology is *creating* the need for new employee skills, as companies race to develop new products and services that depend on computers for production and/or implementation. Similarly, technology not only makes faster decisions possible, it also *mandates* faster decisions. There is no time to ponder and reflect while awaiting a communication from somewhere else in the world.

Tasks.   What needed to be done yesterday differs from what needs to be done today and tomorrow. For example, with the deregulation of the financial services industry, banks suddenly required skilled marketing people in order to compete with each other and with nonbanks. Mechanization and computerization continue to alter all portions of business operations. The avalanche of new markets and customer requirements results in radical product changes. Vanishing trade barriers have spawned "Euromanagers" as replacements for national and regional managers, and the North American Free Trade Agreement may produce the same transmutations on this continent.

People. Employees are demanding challenge and flexibility, giving priority to family concerns and viewing the nature of work in different ways. They change careers far more often than in decades past. And employers are realizing that aligning organizational values and skill needs with personal values is the only way to build productivity.

All these areas are, of course, interrelated. A decision in one area affects all other areas; it is impossible to change just one part of a system. Organizations constantly need to renew, even reinvent, themselves—not simply change a part here and there—in light of new information, new competition, new capabilities, and new developments, both internal and external.

None of these interrelated changes is likely to subside. In fact, they will probably continue to proliferate for some time. Continuity, in the sense of doing the same things in the same way with the same resources, has a short shelf life. Prosperity today is no guarantee of prosperity tomorrow. Wang Laboratories, which pioneered word processors in the 1970s and enjoyed spectacular profits in its early days, failed to anticipate the personal computer revolution in business and filed for Chapter 11 protection in 1992. Digital Equipment and Data General fell into the same kind of trap, becoming so enamored of a "successful" approach that they failed to make fundamental changes to respond to a changing environment.

No organization can thrive forever if it clings stubbornly to old structures, processes, and "never" or "always" principles—*including the principle of never laying off employees.* Even federal, state, and municipal agencies—bastions of lifetime employment and job security—are reducing the size of their workforce and rethinking which services they will continue to offer and at what level.

Various combinations of changes may require an organization to choose between downsizing and death. The unspoken covenant a business used to hand its employees was, "Be loyal, do well, and you can have a job for life." The new, less paternalistic covenant is more likely to be, "You and we will face the market challenges together, but the company can't promise you security—only an opportunity to become more proficient and more valuable." The employees' implied response: "I'll contribute to the best of my ability as long as I'm challenged and growing professionally, I'm compensated fairly, and the company's values mesh with mine."

Both employees and managers know the game has changed. They know that the "job for life" concept is no longer workable, either for businesses or for their staffs. Still, they continue to behave as though downsizing is a shameful anomaly rather than a normal phase in an organization's development. One senior manager of an appliance firm who had to release a large number of competent employees stated that it felt like "an amputation." He was consumed with guilt and a sense of failure. If he had only planned better, had a better strategy, wouldn't he have been able to avoid layoffs?

Probably not. Restructuring, in this case to create a flatter organization and a shift in emphasis from manufacturing to information technology, was necessary in order to meet competitive challenges that the company could not have foreseen. Downsizing was not only inevitable—and a prudent business decision—it was also an experience shared by a majority of the organizations in the same industry. The only difference was in the *way* each organization handled the downsizing and its aftermath.

Denying that downsizing is a fact of organizational life only makes it harder to manage. Afraid to communicate "shameful" news, managers sometimes want to wait until the last moment, sometimes informing employees on Friday afternoon that their jobs will have disappeared by Monday. (More than one firm has accompanied this information with an edict that people leave immediately—their personal belongings to be packed by those remaining and sent by UPS.) Displaced employees, feeling suddenly powerless and betrayed, lose confidence in their ability to find new employment. Management hands them off to outplacement counselors or the unemployment office and refuses to make further eye contact with them. The entire experience becomes so painful that everyone wants to get it over with quickly and then forget about it as soon as possible rather than learn anything about how to do it better next time.

Such morale-destroying cataclysms can be avoided if everyone in the organization—from entry-level employee to CEO and the board— were to take the attitude that downsizing is a fork in the road rather than the end of the road, that is, a transition to be managed like any other, with planning, teamwork, compassion, innovation, and skill.

The prevalence of this attitude determines how well the organization will handle the three key elements described in this book:

- Managing the downsizing process
- Providing for the displaced worker
- Renewing the postdownsized organization

Certainly, shrinking the organization will be difficult, even painful at times. Downsizing involves loss for both employee and employer, and loss is always painful. Acknowledging the importance of that loss is part of the management process. It is possible, however, not only to minimize pain but also to maximize gain. If downsizing is handled effectively, both employees and the organization can learn valuable lessons and skills that can be applied to a variety of situations. Managers, for example, can practice communication, problem solving, and conflict resolution techniques. Employees can learn how to take charge of their own careers and improve their marketability within and outside the organization. The organization, once it has been redesigned and streamlined, can seize the opportunity to put in place, or strengthen, productivity-enhancing strategies such as self-managed work teams and gain-sharing programs. A tree pruner removes not only dead wood but healthy branches as well. Still, the tree does not die; in fact, it becomes healthier—if the pruner is skillful. As chapter 12 indicates, downsizing opens new avenues toward realization of the organization's vision.

THE IMPORTANCE OF DOING IT WELL

Downsizing is a transition that affects all stakeholders in a business: managers, employees, investors, board members, customers, suppliers, and the surrounding community—regional to international.

The impact of downsizing on reputation can reverberate for years. Since organizations are living systems, continually affecting and being affected by both internal and external systems and subsystems, financial impact cannot readily be separated from human effects. For example, if a poorly handled reduction in force results in loss of confidence, commitment, empowerment, and creativity among those who leave and those who remain, the organization will feel the financial consequences in the price of stock, loss of customers, and price negotiations with suppliers. If displaced workers are angry and hostile, they can sabotage production, initiate costly lawsuits, and even do physical damage. Survivors will spend more time protecting their jobs than doing them, and productivity will suffer. When hiring becomes necessary again, the organization may find it difficult to attract talented workers who are in demand—and may have to pay more to get them. Why should I go to work for a company that treats people badly? such candidates are likely to ask themselves.

Managers are shirking their responsibility to their stakeholders if they fail to manage this transition well. They can incur substantial costs and still fail to improve the organization. A 1993 Wyatt Company survey of 450 companies that downsized found that only 60 percent have seen their costs shrink and fewer than half have improved their profits. Of the firms that were targeting productivity increases, only a third have actually achieved it—raising significant questions about the overall value of most currently practiced restructuring, downsizing, and rightsizing strategies. Clearly, there is much to be learned and plenty of room for improvement. Since downsizing is becoming a typical and recurrent event, some organizations are learning how to plan for it, lead it, recover from it, and benefit from it. Competitors who have not mastered this process are at a disadvantage.

Organizations today are likely to go through downsizing more than once as external and internal factors change in unpredictable ways. American businesses have been slashing jobs by more than 2,600 per business day, a rate 5 percent higher than in 1991, when the United States was still in recession. They can choose to make the same mistakes repeatedly or to embrace the challenge and learn from what they do. They can go around in circles or move in an upward spiral, becoming more and more proficient—and thus competitive—each time.

DOWNSIZING AS PART OF CORPORATE STRATEGY

Reducing the size of the workforce is not always a cost-focused reaction to economic problems. It can also be proactive, a pivotal element in the organization's long-term business strategy. Gazing into the crystal ball—which today takes the form of a computer screen as well as a strong intuitive business sense—the organization may determine that it needs to flatten its management hierarchy to make faster decisions and to get its products to the marketplace more quickly. Or it may decide to phase out a division that no longer fits its strategy. An offshore competitor, for example, may have just announced a new

Linear Change

Paradigm Shift

Illustration 1   Linear Change Versus Paradigm Shift

insimilator that will leave Streeter-Haaz's insimilator—its primary product—in the dust, unable to compete in terms of either cost to produce or value to the customer. Streeter-Haaz may even decide that it needs to be in the service business rather than the product business. The result is that the skill mix at Streeter-Haaz will need to change.

Instead of downsizing, companies sometimes refer to *workforce restructuring, resizing, rightsizing,* or *reengineering.* These terms are not always euphemisms designed to soften the blow to employees. They may actually be more accurate terms than *downsizing.* For example, Streeter-Haaz may decide to trim its manufacturing unit 75 percent but simultaneously increase its information sciences unit by 20 percent. While these measures might result in a net downsizing, they also call for hiring a number of new information science specialists.

LINEAR CHANGE OR PARADIGM SHIFT?

Downsizing can be an opportunity to strengthen the existing organization or to transform it into something new. It is essential for management to know which avenue it wishes to pursue: incremental, linear change, which keeps things largely the same but refined and better; or a paradigm shift, which involves a radical new vision of the business and organization (see illustration 1). Table 1 lists strategies

10

Table 1   Strategies for Organizational Transformation: From Linear Change to Paradigm Shift

Linear Change	Paradigm Shift
Downsize *Go on a diet*	REINVENTION/REENGINEERING *Learn new eating habits*
Status quo *Stay with what you know* *Risk adverse*	INNOVATION *Overstep traditional boundaries* *Engage risk*
Protect *If it ain't broke, don't* *fix it* *Success brings success*	LEARN *If it ain't broke, break it and* *do it better* *Success brings failure*
Compliance *Don't mess with what* *we know*	EXPLORATION *Shift to a new game*
Change procedure/rules *Isolated problems*	SHIFT POLICY/SYSTEMS *Systemic issues*
Harbor information	SHARE INFORMATION
Hierarchy	NETWORKING
Control	COMMITMENT
Delegation	EMPOWERMENT
Manager *Do the next right thing*	LEADER *Lead organization to a place* *it wouldn't go by itself*
"Now" decision making *Best today decision*	"FUTURE" DECISION MAKING *How today's choices play out* *in vision, mission, values*
Employees seen as "hands" *Do the job*	EMPLOYEES SEEN AS PEOPLE *Make decisions*
Producer mentality *Search for instructions*	ENTREPRENEUR MENTALITY *Seek results*
Independent	INTERDEPENDENT
Monoculture *Exclusionary rules* *Assimilate* *Loyalty*	DIVERSE CULTURE *Inclusionary rules* *Be effective in own way* *Aloyalty*

for organizational change achieved through linear or paradigmatic shifts.

Paradigms are sets of assumptions that define how an organization and its leaders view the world, set boundaries, select behaviors within these boundaries, and define success. A reversal of rules—for example, asking workers to come up with ideas and advise management—is often an indication of a paradigm shift. If the organization has concluded that it needs a new way of looking at the world and a new set of behaviors, it may be ready for a paradigm shift.

Assessment of the type of change desired should *precede* a downsizing effort, since it is fundamental to the question of which people to keep, which people to let go, and which to hire. Management should bear in mind that revising the culture does not necessarily mean revising the *whole* culture; even within a given organization, businesses can find themselves at different stages of development. A mix of incremental change and paradigm shift might be appropriate. Downsizing is not an isolated event; it is a process, a subsystem interrelated with other business and management subsystems.

KEY QUESTIONS

After assessing whether the change in an organization should be linear or radical, as in a paradigm shift, organizations need to ask themselves some key strategic questions before determining how, when, where, and how much to reduce the workforce.

Long-term strategy questions. What kind of organization do we want to be, given industry trends and the business and economic environment? How do we want to be viewed by our stakeholders? Who will our competitors be and which of their strengths do we need to emulate or exceed? How do we plan to get from where we are to where we want to be? These elemental long-term strategy questions may already have been examined in detail by organizational planners, but they need now to be related to human resource issues.

Business reasons. What, specifically, are the business reasons for reducing staff size? Is leanness the fundamental issue, or is it the need for a new mix of skills?

Customer shifts. Which customers do we want to keep and which can we let go? Should we focus on one or more prime customers? If so, what actions are essential to keep them? Do they expect a specific product or service? Do they have specific deadline and quality standards that must be met?

Staff job skills. Are there specific job skills or core knowledge areas that must be retained or acquired to meet business needs? In some research and development projects or machinery maintenance efforts, for example, core knowledge of the equipment is not easily learned by reading the manuals. Sometimes years of experience passed on from older workers to younger workers constitute the only way to remain competitive. On the other hand, new hires can bring new knowledge and techniques that long-time employees may need to learn.

In the case of mergers and acquisitions, of course, the questions will be somewhat different, as will those asking the questions. This special situation will be discussed in chapter 3.

CONCLUSION

The organizational game has changed, and everyone knows it. When downsizing and restructuring are chosen as one of the main vehicles for moving forward, organizations need to be aware of whether they are making a linear change or a major paradigm shift. The intent of this book is to help managers move through the cataclysm of change in a way that is least harmful to themselves and their workforce and to offer workers a positive revitalization of their work world.

Stuart Aubret opened the door to the conference room on the top floor of Streeter-Haaz's corporate headquarters. As he greeted some of the early arrivals, he thought to himself, They look nervous and worried; I wonder if they know how much these changes are going to affect them, the company, and the employees. Well, we need to move forward. Let's plan this so that our company ends up healthier and revitalized as a result of this very painful process.

2

Pretermination Planning

Stuart Aubret and the organization's vice presidents were meeting in the executive board room. It was 10:00 A.M. on a Friday morning. Outside the sun was shining on the nearby lake. Inside, the mood was gloomy and tense as the executive board once more reviewed the financial reports. The company was in trouble. One of their options was to lay off employees.

They all agreed that implementing a downsizing plan would produce a culture shock that would reverberate throughout the company and the community for many years to come. The organization would never be the same after the first formal downsizing, and each successive restructuring would hammer home the new way of doing business. It was not an action to be lightly considered.

At the close of the meeting, Stuart told the executive group that he was assembling a transition team of senior managers and executives representing product development, manufacturing, sales, human resources, and the controller's office. Also on the team would be the senior vice president who had prodded him the most about long-range planning and who had been his confidante for several years. The senior organizational development specialist would be the final member of the team. Their task would be to identify the crucial questions to be answered before conducting a layoff, find out who could answer them, gather the information, and make recommendations. The information would be brought back to the executive group for final resolution.

The transition team should be appointed by the CEO and should represent the key players in all of the major departments and functions of the company. The people on the team should be respected by the officers, managers, and staff for their competence and their positive vision for the company. With this kind of a team in place and working on the restructuring of the company, the employees and the larger external community will have greater faith in the ability of the organization to come through the major changes with strength. The transition team will meet numerous times and will probably develop task forces to work on specific projects.

The transition team meets several times to discuss their concerns and to formulate key questions. At this early stage, the executives and the transition team experience the same psychological reactions that the supervisors and employees will face later. They wonder about their tenure in the company and whether they will survive the cuts, they grieve the loss of the old days of start-up and maturation, and some start looking for other jobs. They are in the inner circle and can influence the future direction of the company as well as the safety of their own positions. They talk endlessly, and confidentially, about the size of the cuts, the options, and the future of the company. Frequently, these same people who spend three months to a year planning the downsizing of the company and thinking about their own future are incredibly surprised by the strong reaction of the affected supervisors and employees when the news is at last delivered. The difference for employees is that they are involuntarily laid off, usually within a short time period after the announcement, they don't have the option of planning their next career or job moves, and they don't have the option of influencing the future direction of the company or their jobs. The distinction is an important part of the planning process.

At the end of a series of meetings, the transition team develops a checklist of key points and questions duplicated at the end of this chapter. While the "Checklist for Downsizing" reflects a seemingly step-by-step process, it is really iterative and can be set up as independent tasks performed simultaneously or in sequence. The key points are further discussed below.

THE IMPORTANCE OF PLANNING

> The most important step is to decide on the end results and use them as
> the template by which all other steps are measured.
>
> —*President of a West Coast career transition firm*

Companies frequently ask two questions when they think about reducing the size of their staff:

- What needs to be done in order to downsize the workforce?
- How long will it take?

The simple answer to the first question is plan, plan, plan. The complex answer to the second is, it depends. There are some wise old sayings that apply:

Don't throw the baby out with the bath water. Don't simply decide that there will be an across-the-board reduction without looking at the possible loss of key products and key staff.

A stitch in time saves nine. The time spent planning and preparing is onerous for many active and do-it-now managers. Those who believe they can always clean up the mess later will probably spend the next several years sorting through lawsuits, rebuilding the morale and trust of employees, and spending considerable time and money on hiring and training a workforce to replace the competent people they let go.

Conducting a downsizing is a major project. The automobile example in illustration 2 shows three different approaches to downsizing. The last approach, "Downsize by Restructuring," is comparable to taking all of the pieces of the organization—the people, the projects, the products, the structure, the liaisons, and the company culture and history—and restructuring them. The process is revolutionary or evolutionary, depending on the depth of the restructuring, the speed with which it is done, the amount of preparation that has gone into the project, and the vision of the leaders. It involves a large number of decisions made by the company's decision makers and by those who implement the project.

Streeter-Haaz's transition team admits that the key to a successful downsizing is planning—and sometimes a little luck. Planning takes place throughout the key functional areas of the company. The

Just eliminate the most recently installed parts
(last in, first out)

Just remove or sever one major component or department
(lay off everyone in Sam's department)

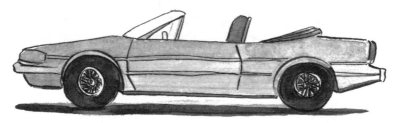

Downsize by restructuring

Illustration 2   Three Ways to Downsize an Automobile

questions the transition team raise will be answered by people who have responsibilities for the following:

- Line management
- Product lines
- Marketing and sales
- Business functions
- Long-range planning
- Organizational development
- Human resources
- Employment
- Labor relations
- Affirmative action
- Employee relations
- Compensation
- Benefits
- Training and development

A Note About Unions

The role of unions is an important one. At this early stage, union issues are handled by the labor relations function, which reviews the negotiated contracts and tries to second-guess how the represented employees and their union will respond. After the layoff decision has been publicly announced, the union representatives become more actively involved. The union's prime vehicle for communication with the management of the organization will continue to be through the labor relations unit.

THE TRANSITION TEAM

The transition team is called many things—the Task Force on Staffing, the Transition Committee, the Workforce Planning Group, and so on. The positive tone of these commonly used designations is intended to keep the task in perspective.

The purpose of downsizing is to effect cost savings through reducing labor expenditures while staying firmly focused on the mission, goals, and corporate values of the organization. A judicious review of the most effective way to use the workforce is as appropriate as the review of capital expenditures and product lines. Managing long-term, complex systems change is a complicated problem that requires the talents and insights of a number of people.

Without a doubt, mergers and acquisitions that try to blend two or more companies have a unique set of challenges. The dominant company generally seeks to impose its way of doing business on the newly purchased organization. An obvious step is to release the bought-out company's senior managers and replace them with those who are in alignment and in allegiance with the purchasing company. Instead of laying off senior managers, they are bought out or asked to leave and invited to make use of a career transition firm to make the shift. The result is still the same. After the new regime is installed, the transition team continues to focus on the key results and outcomes.

With in-house transitions, that is, those not governed by takeover politics but by influential company leaders, senior managers representing the core functions of the organization are essential members of the staffing review committees. Since they are the ones responsible for the quality of the product and the size of the staff required to produce the end result, their viewpoints are essential for the planning process as well as the recovery. Since the business office runs the numbers, they are key to maintaining the perspective on the projected and actual cost savings and expenditures. The human resources department is key to interpreting the policies and providing the internal resources to assist the line managers in making the transitions. Other key managers are those who wield influence despite their title or relative position in the pecking order. An internal or external organizational development specialist is invaluable for maintaining the perspective of the systemwide changes that will be produced.

The transition team is the inner group that funnels the direction of the plans made for downsizing and questions the answers delivered by others.

COMPANY MISSION AND FUTURE DIRECTION

Most employees don't know the mission of the company they work for and many don't care. It typically becomes important to them only when they're unsure that what they are doing is in the mainstream of company business or that it is essential to the future direction of the company—in other words, if they are suddenly worried that they will lose their jobs.

Mergers and acquisitions make everyone nervous. What will be the new direction of this organizational marriage? What functions will stay? which ones will go? and more important, who will stay and who will become redundant? At this point, the mission and future direction become extraordinarily important to everyone in the company. And as soon as it is publicly known, it also becomes important to the competitors, stockholders, vendors, and numerous affiliated organizations.

In both merger and nonmerger shifts, a clearly phrased and frequently cited mission statement helps the organization focus on its key efforts. It also provides the business reason to lay off employees whose functions don't fit the mission or the new direction of the company. The well-publicized mission statement also serves to ease the transition of employees to new positions within the organization because their skills and abilities are needed in another project or product line.

DOWNSIZING AND THE COMPANY CULTURE

How does downsizing fit into the company's culture? What culture should be fostered in the "new and improved" organization? There has been a lot written in the past ten to fifteen years about a company's culture. Generally, every company, every organization, every division and work group develops its own work style. People coming fresh into the organization often remark on *how* people communicate with one another, *how* they follow rules, and *who* they hold up as heroes. If the current culture is desirable and the company wants to maintain it, then layoffs will inevitably be handled in the same style. If the intent is to change the culture and the values of the organization, managing layoffs should be congruent with the new style. The smaller the change, the quicker will be the move toward assimilation and "normalcy." However, almost every downsizing produces a shift in the thinking patterns of employees and managers. The resulting organizational, business, and culture shifts are talked about for years. Unless the culture change makes sense to people and unless they want it to occur, morale and productivity will be problematic.

RATIONALE FOR DOWNSIZING

In brief, downsizing alters the traditional, established way of doing business regardless of whether it is a nonprofit organization, educational and government institution, or private industry. The longer the organization has been in business, the more established are the traditions and the links between staff members, and the more resistant everyone is to change. To disrupt the business by laying off a few or a lot of workers is to "kill off" some of the vital members of the work family. The rationale of focusing (or refocusing) on the company's core mission and establishing clear-sighted future directions needs to be clearly and frequently stated to employees.

WHAT TO CALL "IT"

The words used to describe the reduction in an organization's workforce are numerous. The most frequently used by the media is *layoff.* However, to many companies and their labor organizations, a layoff is a negotiated agreement that states that union employees will be hired back on a preferential basis and in reverse order of layoff. Companies have come up with an extraordinary number of words and phrases to name the action of reducing the size of their workforce. Some examples: redeployment, redundancy and retrenchment (frequently used in Canada and England), reduction in force, workforce reduction, downsizing, rightsizing, slimming, trimming, cutting out the fat, cutback, pinkslipped. *Training Magazine* (Gordon, 1991) published a list of "genuine corporate euphemisms for firing people: career-change opportunity, decruitment, degrowing, dehiring, destaffing, personnel surplus reduction, redirectment, reorganization, skill mix adjustment, and workforce imbalance correction" (p. 42). What it is called is important to establishing the tone of the downsizing and even to maintaining the morale of the ongoing workforce. Nobody wants to work for a lean and mean organization, one that dumps people. People don't like to be redeployed either, but it does add dignity to the process and takes some of the sting out of being fired.

OPTIONS AND COSTS

There are at least twenty distinctly different options for reducing the size and/or the cost of the workforce, some of which are presented in

Involuntary
Termination

Hiring
Freeze

Attrition

Voluntary
Termination

Early
Retirement

Illustration 3   Options for Downsizing

illustration 3. They can be roughly divided into four categories: reducing the inward flow of new employees, increasing the number of departures, reducing the cost of current employees, and increasing the flexibility and internal transfer of staff. Some can be managed over a short time period; others are long-term strategies. Some are single-shot strategies, and others can be done simultaneously. The options are discussed in greater detail in chapter 3.

What will be the financial impact of each of the options? What cost savings are required? Labor costs are frequently an organization's largest expenditure. Most school districts, academic institutions, research organizations, and government agencies estimate that the cost of salaries, benefits, and retirement comprises 75 to 90 percent of an organization's budget. Therefore, if those expenditures can be reduced, there will obviously be a cost savings. Strategies are created that implement several end results. Attrition and hiring freezes reduce the number of employees by reducing the number who stay in the organization as well as reducing the number who newly enter the workforce.

IMPACT ON STAFF

What are the criteria for determining who gets laid off? Every organization wants to fire its poor performers. However, selectively laying them off is almost guaranteed to invite legal action. Managing performance problems is a separate and distinct concern that still needs to be handled through the conventional performance appraisal and dismissal process. It is part of the long-term solution to reducing the workforce.

The essence of this question is to establish clear-cut, defensible criteria for identifying who will be terminated. The answer will determine if certain groups of people are being discriminated against or even if there is an appearance of discrimination. In either case, there is a strong likelihood that lawsuits will result. There are certain standard reasons for laying off employees that are not related to personal performance.

Last hired, first fired. The unions have traditionally preferred criteria based on seniority. The issue is job security and living up to promises made by the company to reward employees for their years of service during employment and to provide pension benefits after they retire. The more senior employees generally have a higher salary, are older, and have spent more years with the company. Based on most companies' retirement plans, they are the ones who will receive the higher pension benefits. Based on traditional hiring practices, the older worker generally has a more difficult time finding another job, while the younger worker is perceived to be more job mobile. The precedent of laying off by seniority has been well established and is generally held up in court as being fair to all employees. Seniority is also an "objective" measure, and objectivity is highly prized by lawyers and judges.

Terminating a percentage across the entire company.   Occasionally, a company will announce that there will be an across-the-board cut of 5 percent of their entire workforce. The challenge is to identify which employees or job functions constitute the 5 percent and to ensure that the impact on older workers, minorities, and employees in protected classes is not unfair.

Eliminating a single division, function, plant, or work site.   The Fusion Energy Division at Los Alamos National Laboratory in New Mexico recently received severe budget cuts from the Department of Energy and so the decision was made to close out the function. Because the funding for fusion energy dried up, Los Alamos had a defensible business reason for eliminating an entire division. They had a selective layoff that focused on only the one division. One of their first priorities was to try to inplace scientists, engineers, technicians, and administrative and secretarial staff into other divisions within the laboratory. Those that could not be placed were offered retraining and/or career transition services. Because Los Alamos is the prime employer in northern New Mexico, there was a strong potential impact on the surrounding communities and the state. The final result was that only a small number of people left the company.

So now the decision needs to be made: Should there be an across-the-board cut or a selective layoff? Will all departments be required to lay off 5 percent of employees, or will some be asked to fire 10 percent and others 3 percent? It still comes down to numbers. What wage reductions, including benefits, perks, and their related financial measures, are required? How many people need to be dismissed in order to meet cost savings goals? Whose salaries should be included in the averaging process? Obviously, this process demands a lot of number crunching and multiple scenario development before any final decisions can be made.

Profiling Employees

Based on the guidelines for each scenario, profile the employees who will be targeted for layoff as well as those who will make up the continuing strategic workforce. Use of an employee profile checklist such as that presented on page 24 will be helpful in providing a quick snapshot of your organization's workforce.

Employee Profile Checklist

❑ Ethnicity
How many employees are in each ethnic group?
What is the ethnic ratio?

❑ Are they in a protected group?
- Disabled
- Vietnam veteran
- Older worker

❑ Age range
- Under 40
- Age 41–50
- Age 51–60
- Over 60

❑ Gender

❑ Years of service
- 0–1 year
- 2–5 years
- 6–10 years
- 11–20 years
- 21–30 years
- More than 30 years

❑ Salary levels

❑ Job titles

❑ Departments or functions represented

❑ Levels of responsibility

❑ Are they supervisors or managers?

❑ Are they represented by a union?

❑ Skills and abilities
What skills and abilities are represented?
Are there certain job skills that can be eliminated or that must be retained?

❑ The ultimate questions
Which ones should be let go and which should be retained?
What will be the impact if they or their functions are removed?

Affirmative Action Concerns

For the past few years, organizations have targeted minorities, women, the disabled, and veterans in their hiring programs. Under the last-hired–first-fired layoff strategy, these individuals are among the first to be targeted for dismissal. The affirmative action programs for a company need to be factored into the long-range plans as well as into the layoff strategies.

Job Skill and Experience Concerns

A crucial question to determine is whether there are specific job skills or core knowledge areas that must be retained for the ongoing health of the organization. For example, in some research and development projects or machinery maintenance efforts, the core knowledge of the equipment is not easily learned by reading the manuals or by new employees. Sometimes, years of experience passed on from older workers to younger workers is the only way to remain competitive. The opposite can also be true: A company that has decided to eliminate its shipping and receiving department probably does not need its warehousing, shipping, and receiving clerks.

IMPACT ON THE STRATEGIC WORKFORCE

There is an assumption that those who retain their jobs will be so grateful that they will be more productive, or, that they will be so worried about losing their jobs in the next round of layoffs that they will also be more productive. It's the implied carrot-and-stick psychology of motivating workers. However, physical and emotional factors such as exhaustion from doing two jobs, worry and guilt as a result of the "missed bullet syndrome," anger at the company for firing friends and colleagues while giving the CEO a big pay raise, gratitude for getting a regular paycheck, and insecurity about not knowing where the company is headed all play a role in how well the ongoing strategic workforce performs. This will be discussed more thoroughly in chapters 11 and 12.

The impact on organizational structure is also a factor. What departments will be affected? What functions may or may not be eliminated or merged? How will the functions be performed and managed after downsizing? As with individual workers, the work of two or more departments can be radically affected by restructuring. They are often collapsed into single units and still expected to perform the work efficiently and effectively. Training and retraining employees, redefining roles and responsibilities, reexamining the work flow and production output, and redefining the power structure are all part of the organizational restructuring. It takes time and thoughtfulness and planning. This subject will be covered in chapters 11 and 12.

PERSONNEL POLICIES

Personnel policies are created to establish guidelines on corporate and employee behavior. Refer to the checklist below to review important personnel policies that need to be considered when planning for a downsizing initiative.

Personnel Policies Checklist

- ❑ What internal policies govern voluntary and involuntary dismissals?
  - Managers
  - Exempt employees
  - Employees on commission schedules
  - Nonexempt, nonunion employees
  - Union workers
  - Temporary staff
  - Contract staff
  - Faculty
  - Special appointments
  - Employees on special leave (e.g., leave without pay, sabbaticals)
  - Employees on disability leave
  - Employees with unique contracts
  - Others
- ❑ What union contract agreements exist regarding layoffs?
- ❑ Can employees volunteer to be laid off and receive a severance payment? Is there an early retirement provision?
- ❑ What policies govern the transition of employees from one classification of work to another?
- ❑ If clerical employees are now expected to learn budget operations, should their job classifications, salary, or overtime rates be changed?

- ❑ Will layoff impact any union agreement or organizational policy?
- ❑ Will some employees move from management to nonmanagement positions?
- ❑ How will this impact their salary, benefits, managerial perks, bonuses?

LEGAL IMPACT

What are the federal and state legal requirements for downsizing a company and for affecting particular groups of workers? Major new legislation now affects all employee decisions: the Worker Adjustment and Retraining Notification Act (WARN), the Age Discrimination in Employment Act (ADEA), and the Americans With Disabilities Act (ADA). CEOs and human resource managers need to know what they must do to keep themselves out of legal hot water. Those who wander into a downsizing without regard for legal concerns will spend years resolving the resulting grievances and suits. Chapter 4 deals more extensively with the federal laws that impact employers.

SEVERANCE PACKAGES

Severance packages are routine for most companies for their management and executive levels. The most extensive review of financial packages given to exiting employees is in the Right Associates (1990) book *Severance*. They also have an executive report that highlights their findings based on surveys taken at the annual conferences of the Society for Human Resource Management and other personnel meetings. Severance packages have become the common name for financial offerings, such as money for a defined time period, extended benefits, or assistance in purchasing major items such as cars, that are given to exiting employees (usually managers) to encourage them to leave the organization. Financial deals offered to employees who take advantage of early retirement are another form of severance package.

TRANSITION SERVICES

An enormous business has been developed to help corporations with the challenge of assisting their ex-employees in finding new positions.

These transition services, actually part of a severance package, are offered to specific groups of employees (e.g., executives and managers) or to all employees in varying levels of service. The two major service providers are the community-based Private Industry Councils (PICs), which are funded by the federal Job Training Partnership Act (JTPA), and the private career transition firms. There are numerous other providers as well: nonprofit organizations, religious and community groups, and private career counselors. Some individuals seek and pay for assistance on their own. These resources are discussed extensively in chapters 4, 5, and 6.

EXTERNAL IMPACT

Many companies myopically focus on their internal reorganization and their internal problems, forgetting that their actions affect their customers, competitors, stockholders, and the community, from regional to international. The message an organization gives to the world can affect future sales as well as public relations. Two stories highlight this issue: the story of Roger, and the story of the Bank of New England.

Roger

For the past year, four owners of some residentially zoned acreages have been working closely with Roger, a civil design engineer in an architectural and construction firm, to lay out the plans for the development of 30 houses. Roger spent hours designing the streets, the sewers and water system, and the general landscaping to meet city requirements. The property owners were in frequent contact with him and had developed a rapport and trust. Then one day, one of the partners called to get some cost estimate information from him.

"May I speak with Roger?"

"He's gone. Laid off yesterday."

"Oh. Who is taking over his work?"

"His boss is."

"Can I speak to his boss?"

"He isn't here right now."

It took three phone calls to get a response. And then not only did the boss not have the answers, he couldn't interpret the information that had already been put together. Was his boss incompetent? More likely he was just having to work extra hard to pick up the projects that had been started by several of his former design engineers. What was the impact on his customers? They were dismayed and annoyed. The project was delayed several weeks until the person who was to take over could come up to speed, and property owners were charged for this learning time. If this small example is extended to a larger effort with many more people involved and more choices available, that business might find itself losing customers.

From the client's perspective, if one part of the business can no longer deliver the goods or services, then perhaps all of the affiliated businesses are in trouble.

The Bank of New England

When financial problems forcing a reduction in force at the Bank of New England were widely publicized in 1990, commercial customers were doubly hurt. One customer said her business was doing just fine; however, her suppliers wanted their products paid for immediately and didn't want checks written on the bank's accounts. She could no longer place telephone orders and expect immediate shipment. She was required to obtain a cashier's check from another bank, send the check to the supplier, and wait until the check was received before the shipment could be made. To compound the matter, her customers were becoming dissatisfied because they had to wait longer than usual for their orders. The bank lost a good customer. The merchant's credit diminished in the eyes of her supplier, and her customer service credibility diminished in the eyes of her customers.

An analysis of the impact on clients is essential in order to keep the clients' business.

CONCLUSION

The ultimate question is, if we follow this scenario, will it be in alignment with the organization's mission and with the strategic plan? Will it dismiss people with dignity so that they, the company, the customer, and the community can move forward in as positive a manner as possible? The responses to these questions provide guidance for the kind of layoff that will meet the company's strategic plan for the future and determine the next steps the company will take. Analysis at this stage of the layoff pays off. If the scenario doesn't work on paper, it won't work on people.

Checklist for Downsizing

❑ The transition team
Are there representatives from all of the following organizational units?
- Functional units
- Business units
- Human resources
- Key managers

❑ Company mission and future direction
How will downsizing impact the mission and future direction of the company?
What direction should the company take in the future?
Will the mission of the organization change?
What business should the organization be in?
How does downsizing fit into the company's culture?
What culture should be fostered in the "new and improved" organization?

❑ Rationale and name for downsizing
What are the business reasons for reducing staff size?
What other cost-cutting measures is the company putting into place?
What will the downsizing be called?
What will the organization say publicly about the downsizing?

❑ Options
Are there optional strategies for reducing staff size?

❑ Costs
What will be the financial impact of each of the options?
What cost savings are required?

❑ Impact on staff
What criteria will be used to determine who will be laid off?
What is the profile of the dismissed employees?
What will be the impact on affirmative action and cultural diversity?
How will the criteria impact
- Union staff
- Nonexempt staff
- Exempt staff
- Management
- Executives

What will be the impact on the ongoing, strategic workforce?
How will the company maintain the productivity and morale of the ongoing workforce?

❏ Impact on organizational structure
What departments will be affected?
What functions will be affected?
How will the functions be performed and managed after downsizing?

❏ Personnel policies
What internal policies govern voluntary and involuntary dismissal?
- Managers
- Exempt employees
- Employees on commission schedules
- Nonexempt, nonunion employees
- Union workers
- Temporary staff
- Contract staff
- Faculty
- Special appointments
- Employees on special leave (e.g., leave without pay, sabbaticals)
- Employees on disability leave
- Employees with unique contracts
- Others

❏ Unions
What union contract agreements exist regarding layoffs?

❏ Voluntary layoff
Can employees volunteer to be laid off and still receive severance pay?

❏ Classification changes
What policies govern the transition of employees from one classification of work to another?

❏ Legal impact
What are the federal and state requirements for voluntary and involuntary dismissals? plant closing notices?
Is there any evidence of unlawful discrimination or the appearance of unlawful discrimination?
What are the legal rights of employees according to internal company policies?

❏ Severance packages and other monetary or perk options
What is currently offered to nonmanagement employees?
What is currently offered to management employees?
Does the exiting package need to be changed?
What special "sweeteners" might be offered for those signing waivers?

❏ Transition services
What kind of transition services will be available?
- Executives
- Middle managers
- First-line supervisors
- Hourly staff (administrative and blue collar)
- Union employees

Who will provide the transition services?
- Internal human resources staff
- Local Private Industry Council (PIC)
- Local career counselors on site
- Local or regional career transition firm
- National or international career transition firm

❏ External impact
What will be the impact on the customer, client, or supplier?
How will the downsizing impact the community?
How will the downsizing impact competitors?
What will the stockholders say or do?
How will the media report the news?
Who will be the prime company contact for each of the above groups?
What message about the company will be given to each of these groups?

3

Options For Downsizing

Elizabeth Lamond, Senior Vice President of Long-range Planning, was sitting in her darkened office on the top floor of the Streeter-Haaz building. It was after 9:00 P.M., and the city lights were sparkling. How many lights were out there? There must be a million, she thought. She had been after Stuart Aubret for months to give her the go-ahead to initiate a succession planning and workforce forecasting system. Now it looked as though she was going to be up to her neck in workforce review. But it wasn't quite the way she wanted it. She was now a member of the transition team charged with examining the optional strategies for laying off employees.

She looked at the stack of files, booklets, and folders piled high on her desk. There seemed to be as many files as there were lights in the city. There were news clippings describing staff reductions at IBM, Pan Am, and Apple Computer. There were charts illustrating her own organization's attrition rate. There were compensation studies covering the current practices within their industry. A large red bound book was crammed with descriptions of benefits and perks. A copy of the WARN legislation covered with yellow highlighter was attached to the fancy brochure that outlined a comprehensive career transition program.

Everything on the desk had something to do with the downsizing that she and the task force had been asked to plan. So many options. Where would she start?

OPTIONS FOR REDUCING
THE SIZE OF THE WORKFORCE

Downsizing has a tremendous impact on employees, the community, the business product, the balance sheet, and the company culture. Once downsizing is chosen as the direction the company will take, there are a number of short-term options to consider:

- Normal attrition
- Hiring options
- Wage options
- Work hour options
- Voluntary retirement options
- Termination options

The options within each category should be considered for increasing cost savings to the employer. However, monetary cost isn't the only factor. After all, when an employer closes a company, there is no opportunity to increase business and job opportunities. Each option will differentially affect the company, the management, the employee, and the community. Each of the strategies is described below, followed by a consideration regarding the impact it will have and the advantages and disadvantages to those who are affected.

Normal Attrition

Attrition is the natural and normal process of employees quitting their jobs, retiring, or dying. The end result for the employer, if these employees are not replaced, is a reduction in the workforce. Public agencies such as schools, colleges, and government organizations tend to have a low attrition rate in the 6 to 12 percent per year range. High-tech and fast-food firms traditionally have had very high turnover or attrition rates of 30 to 150 percent per year.

Attrition is seldom used as a downsizing tool by itself. It is usually coupled with one or more of the other options described below.

The advantages and disadvantages of using attrition as a downsizing measure are essentially the same as for voluntary layoffs. For companies that have been in business for several years, the attrition rate is fairly predictable. However, it's hard to identify in advance who is going to leave since the highly skilled as well as the less capable say

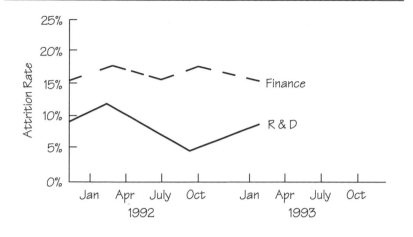

Ilustration 4 **Attrition Rates for Two Different Departments Within the Same Organization**

goodbye. As shown in illustration 4, attrition rates can be different for different parts of the same organization. Studies can be conducted to identify those in each age group within each department. This quasi-actuarial data can give a rough guide as to which people, professional categories, and departments can expect the greatest number of retirements and deaths over each succeeding year. Voluntary quit rates for each department can also be rated. Thus, there is some predictability that can be used to allow parts of the organization to obtain naturally a low level of attrition and then be absorbed or dismantled. This presumes that the corporate managers have looked to the future to decide which parts of the organization they want to strengthen and which to diminish.

Hiring Options

HIRING SLOWDOWN.   Sometimes hiring slowdowns are called *frosts, soft freezes,* or *temporary freezes.* The intent is to slowly reduce the number of new employees by demanding that all hiring offers go through an increasingly lengthy review process. Possibly, all new hires would have to be approved by the company president. The impact on managers is to signal that there will probably be a hiring freeze in the near future. They know that if they have someone they want to hire, they will have to do it immediately and with more justification. Managers and their staff, who are anticipating the additional support a new employee, will begin to feel frustrated and to complain about all the red tape. Potential new employees may wonder why the organization is so slow to hire them and begin to seek other employment options to cover their bases. Old-timers know that the slowdown will last only a short while and will result either in a freeze or a thaw in hiring.

The advantage to senior management is that it gives them time to consider what kind of staff they want to hire, what part of their business they want to expand or contract, what job skills they want to emphasize, and how much wage cost savings they really need. It is also a signal to the board of directors that management is paying attention to profit-and-loss statements and taking steps to shore up the bottom line. With downsizings and layoffs now a norm in business, a hiring slowdown probably will not be noticed—and certainly not reported—by the business publications. It is unlikely to affect stock prices, much less the sale or purchase of stock. The positive impact within the company is that it forewarns employees to pay attention to their productivity.

HIRING FREEZE.   Hiring freezes have been used by most companies as a short-term solution to what is viewed as a temporary problem. Simply put, the company decides not to hire any new employees until further notice. Here's a possible scenerio of what can result once a hiring freeze has been imposed:

> Problems immediately arise. With turnover running 30 percent a year for the manager of a major product line, new employees are needed to staff the assembly line. Without a new crew, the manager will have to shut down one line, accept a decrease in quality, eliminate one shift, and possibly create time delays for customers. So the manager appeals for an exemption from the policy.

> In the meantime, the head of the legal section has one employee out on long-term disability and another out on a one-year leave of absence to get a company-supported advanced degree. The division head asks the department head to review a large number of employee profiles for possible discrimination in the event of a layoff. The department head needs more professional staff and appeals for an exception in this case to make a hire.

In hiring freezes, there are usually exceptions that are included in the language. The wording is frequently phrased as follows:

"Exceptions will be made based on the unique skills and abilities needed by the requesting department," or "All hiring requests will be reviewed by the CEO" (or the department manager, or the product manager, or senior manager). As time passes, hiring freezes thaw a little at a time, usually without any policy change. The staffing level swings from overextended to too low to back-to-normal and, not infrequently, to a higher level than it was before.

The disadvantage of a hiring freeze is that it is difficult to control which departments and which functions will incur staff losses or how large they will be. The departments with the greatest turnover may not be the departments where an employer wants to reduce staff. In the workforce itself, the immediate impact is to create a little more fear about job security. Employees become more reluctant to leave the company since they might not be able to come back—even if they don't want to come back. Or, they anticipate that there will be layoffs accompanied by buyouts, severance pay, or other financial rewards for leaving. Those who thought about retiring this year now may hold off a while longer.

The more frequent the hiring freezes and subsequent thaws, the more comfortable employees are with them. "This too will pass" becomes the byword. Some companies opt to have partial freezes, that is, they eliminate all new hiring in a particular department, product line, or location.

The advantage of a hiring freeze, of course, is that it reduces the size of the existing workforce. Employees feel a little nervous about their jobs, depending on the frequency and usual outcome of freezes, but on the whole, they're happy that they are among the employed workers.

Wage Options

In this series of options, *wages* include salary, benefits, and perquisites (perks). Traditionally, it is the second phase of cost containment measures used by companies. It doesn't do anything to reduce the size of the workforce; however, if the goal is cost containment, the following options can be considered.

REDUCE PERCENTAGE OF PAY INCREASES. The U.S. Department of Energy (DOE) contracts with a number of private and public companies throughout the country. Every winter the ritual of next October's raises begins. Each contractor assembles comparative data, DOE looks into its funding coffers, and both sides start the new round of salary negotiations. By summer, employees and managers are taking bets on the percentage of the facility's overall wage increment. By the end of August or even September, the "number" is released and managers quickly move to manage the salaries, including the size of the increase each employee receives. For the past several years, the size of the percentage has decreased, thus reducing the annual increase at a sizable cost savings to the federal government.

The disadvantage is that contract agency managers have less money to reward their high performers and less to award all of their employees. One of the recurring arguments to increase the level of the annual raise is to keep pace with the salaries offered by competitors. They want to keep good employees happy and productive in their current job and minimize the possibility of losing some of them to other potentially better-paying organizations.

Salary increases in all companies have been a standard measure of self-worth and company-worth for many years. In good years, the percentage has been high and employees have expected to receive 8 to 15 percent increases. Anything less has been viewed as a negative indicator of current and future value to the company. During recessionary times, when the percentage of pay increases shrinks and increasing numbers of employees are laid off, many employees consider themselves lucky to receive any increase at all. The end result, though, is that many employees do a lot of grumbling about their "low" salaries and their small raises and begin questioning the size of the senior managers' salaries. If the CEO and other senior managers receive large increases while employees do not, the morale of the workforce starts to decline. Employees may stay put, but they start worrying about the stability of their jobs.

DEFER DATE OF PAY INCREASES.   In both 1991 and 1992, the State of California declared a multibillion dollar deficit. While the federal government is not required to balance its budget every year, the State of California is. One of the ways that the state can reduce costs is to reduce funding of state employees' salaries. The University of California chose a multifaceted approach to handling the budget reduction. One facet was to defer all pay increases for its 88,000 faculty and staff for a minimum of one year.

The others included raising tuition rates, hosting an early retirement program, and laying off staff, as well as reducing expenditures such as those for travel. With subsequent budget declines, then-President David P. Gardner publicly announced that all executive-level staff would receive no pay increases. Several weeks later, he announced that employees would receive no merit increases for a year. The early announcement of the no pay increases for executives was not only a smart public relations move (the underlying message was that the executives cared enough about their public responsibility and their staff to cut their own salaries first), but it also eased the comments from staff who were later told that they would not receive merit pay increases. The advantage to the University, as an employer, is that by deferring pay raises, they can reduce the cost of salaries and thereby effect at least a partial cost-cutting measure. It also means that they do not need to lay off as many employees or tighten budgets even more stringently.

From an employee viewpoint, it is a mild measure. Those who are not laid off can say, "Well, at least I still have my job and the same income I had before. I can live with it." Further, it is perceived to be fair and just: All employees—managers and staff—share the wage deferment.

Wage deferments also signal to company managers that economic times are expected to be tight for at least six months or longer and that they will be expected to effect other cost saving measures as well. The concern, always, is that the employer will potentially lose some of their employees to organizations that pay better salaries and offer more perks.

FREEZE WAGES. Just as the name implies, all wages are frozen at their current level, with no stated time for a guaranteed increase. Currently, there is new talk among employers and compensation managers: "Who says that employees have to get salary increases every year?" "Where is it written that companies should give an annual cost-of-living increase to their employees?" Many union contracts, of course, have it in writing that their members will receive an annual increase. And the federal government's retirement programs award their former employees with cost-of-living adjustments. It was only in the "flush fifties" through the "golden eighties"—in the heady rush of good jobs, good salaries, and a strongly rising economy—that wage earners saw annual increases on a regular basis. Perhaps in the nineties, more

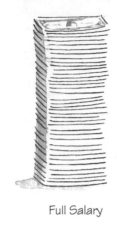

Full Salary   5% Cut   10% Cut

**Ilustration 5   Cost of Maintaining a Stable-Sized Workforce
by Revising Salaries**

companies will reevaluate this annual ritual of guaranteed increases, annual bonuses, and more perks. *Fortune* magazine (July 12, 1993) published an article, "Jobs in America: When Will You Get a Raise?" which cites the increasing number of attaboy awards and the decreasing number of bonuses and pay raises throughout corporate America.

REDUCE WAGES.   Indeed, some firms are requesting that their employees take a pay cut in order to keep their jobs and the company afloat. Illustration 5 shows the cost of maintaining a stable sized workforce by revising salaries. Another variation was proposed by the California State Employees Association to temporarily reduce the threat of layoffs of Alameda County employees. They agreed that their members would work two days without pay in order to save the jobs of approximately 2,000 employees for another six months.

REDUCE BENEFITS AND PERKS.   The cost of health care and benefits has been spiraling upward faster than the rate of inflation and faster than a company's ability to keep up with them. Some companies are offering fewer benefits, reconsidering their offer of lifetime benefits after retirement, and asking employees to ante up more of their own money to cover the costs. During the early nineties' holiday seasons, catering businesses were in a tailspin because of the reduction in company-sponsored holiday parties. Fewer parties, smaller bonuses, and reduced benefits are all ways that the company uses to save money and possibly jobs.

The major advantage to companies for reducing salaries, bonuses, benefits, and perks is obvious—it's a direct cost saving. Both companies and employees benefit if it means that the organization can manage its cost flow and employees still maintain their jobs. With the dramatic increase in two-income families, some employees can cushion their standard of living expenses better than when they were just a one-income family. However, many two-paycheck families have major healthcare, education, and housing expenses that demand their full incomes. Unfortunately, single wage earners and single parent families suffer the most.

For most employers, it is a two-sided option: There is the promise of better days to come and the potential to offer employees full-scale wages again. There is also the possibility that they will be able to hire employees at lower starting salary level rates.

The disadvantage is that the shift from reduction in pay increases to reduction in actual salary can mean that employees will seek better paying, more stable salaries in other firms. In fact, the wage reductions might produce enough worry and concern in the workforce that their productivity will decrease along with their salary.

Work Hour Options

REQUEST VOLUNTARY REDUCTIONS IN WORK TIME. The president of a high-tech equipment manufacturer asked his permanent, nonunion employees if any of them wanted to voluntarily reduce the amount of time they worked. This was well received by employees who had been demanding dependent care responsibilities or had nonwork projects they wanted to pursue. Employees who work more than 50 percent time keep their full benefits and their status as permanent employees. However, salary and rate of seniority are prorated based on the amount of time worked.

With this option, employees make the decision, subject to management approval, to reduce their work time. Employees feel positive about being given the choice, and this has a positive impact on the organization. Three groups of employees are likely to take advantage of a reduction from full-time work to part-time work: those with dependent care responsibilities, those who are close to retiring and want to ease out slowly, and those who want more time to pursue their own activities. The traditional work schedule of eight-hour days, forty-hour weeks, from 8:00 A.M. to 5:00 P.M. with an hour for lunch is still strong, although fraying around the edges.

The overwhelming advantage to a company that extends the offer to employees to voluntarily reduce work hours and salary is that the company is perceived as being responsive to employee needs. One of the criteria for *Working Woman* magazine's annual list of "best companies to work for" is time flexibility.

Managers feel both positive and negative about work hour flexibility, depending on their style, how their own salary is determined, and the workload of their employees. On the positive side, they can maintain control of the work flow by denying or affirming the request or by suggesting alternatives. On the negative side, if they are used to a full-time staff and are unwilling or not able to reduce the number of hours, they sometimes feel badgered into creating alternative work schedules. Another major disadvantage is that when management notices that the work is being done in less time and with reduced staff, they turn a temporary reduction in staff size into a permanent reduction. That's only one part of the dilemma. The other is that if a manager's salary is based on the size of the operation and the number of staff, there is a strong disincentive to approve reduced work schedules. The advantage of short-term cost savings comes at the expense of the manager's future earnings.

One other disadvantage is not only that few employees may voluntarily reduce their work time but also those who do request shorter hours won't necessarily be the ones who are less productive. The offset is that usually management reserves the right to approve or disapprove who can work part-time and which functions can be handled on a reduced basis. The challenge for managers is to figure out the work needs and the common hours when a core group of employees must be available to service the public or meet in-house requirements and then to keep the schedules straight.

OFFER VOLUNTARY LEAVES OF ABSENCE WITHOUT PAY. Some employees need time off, with or without pay, to handle dependent care needs, to go to school, or to sail around the world. Some want just a few weeks off; rarely will someone request a year. Those who request a temporarily reduced work schedule want to be guaranteed that they can have their job back and at the same salary. Usually only a small number of employees take the offer of time off without pay. One business unit in AT&T has offered a special employee leave of absence (without pay) program for a period of up to two years. While the program is still too young to analyze, the short-term results show that employees like the option and the chance for renewal. The commitment to return to work at the same pay level (but not the same job) offers a safety net for those who want a sabbatical or an almost risk-free opportunity to expand their career sights.

The overall advantages and disadvantages of leave without pay are intertwined.

If the employee doesn't return, it is

- A plus in terms of salary savings
- A plus for holding a position open and not losing it in permanent budget cuts
- A plus for trying out another internal person in the position on a temporary basis
- A minus in terms of getting as much work done as before
- A minus for permanently promoting or making a lateral transfer of another employee

If the employee keeps asking for extensions, it is

- A plus for salary savings
- A plus for keeping the position open
- A minus for keeping the employee loyal and visible in the organization
- A minus for developing the on-leave employee's career capabilities
- A minus if the employee becomes less loyal and/or less productive because of his or her reduced time and effort commitments

If the employee comes back and the position has been filled by others, it is

- A plus for creating new job opportunities for the returning employee (perhaps a better position will be found)
- A minus if more competent people have been doing the work and the only position the absentee job holder can assume is that one function
- A minus if there are no other comparable positions at the same salary and the other employees holding down the jobs temporarily have to give up their work

If an employer has to hire someone to do the job, it is

- A plus if the employer can try a person out in this position before offering him or her a permanent job
- A minus for more expenditures
- A minus if the new person can only be offered a temporary position

SHUT DOWN THE FACILITY TEMPORARILY.   Almost everyone loves the idea of taking two weeks off at Christmas or Hanukkah to be with family and then taking another week off over the long President's holiday weekend to go skiing. However, only a few people want to take vacation without pay.

The advantage to the company of a temporary shut-down is that it reduces the cost of salaries by approximately 25 percent per month for every week the company is shut down. Also reduced are the cost of heat and electricity, cafeteria services, and security. For many companies, this is the ideal time to do plant maintenance—at day rates, with no expensive overtime or off-shift pay differentials. While some employees like to work the time between Christmas and New Year's Day, most prefer to take some time off over the holidays.

The disadvantage is that it does reduce take-home pay for employees. It also potentially reduces the amount of money flowing into the community's stores over the big holiday buying season, and that affects the area's financial well-being and its ability to sustain the economy.

REQUIRE INVOLUNTARY REDUCTION IN WORK HOURS.   Examples of involuntary work-time reduction include company mandates that employees take time off work every other Friday or that they take the last day of the month off without pay. In essence, the work time has been reduced by approximately five percent for every day per month not worked—and with it the cost of doing business.

This is a relatively easy way to reduce costs. Everyone keeps his or her job. It is perceived as a fair and equitable cut in pay for everyone. Employees take a day or two off each month and just tighten their financial belt a little. Most younger employees as well as those closer to retirement feel rewarded by getting a little more time off. For many, time is a more important commodity than money—as long as it's only a small change in their income.

The downside is that there is still work to be done and the office schedule is more complicated now that people are working different days. Further, senior managers might enjoy the cost savings and perceive that their employees are just as productive as they were on the full schedule and decide to maintain the reduced schedule. The ones who seem least satisfied are the managers who frequently must work a full schedule. As one manager at a manufacturing facility put it, "I was working a fifty-hour workweek—and getting paid for forty hours—before the company bosses gave everyone a day off every month. And I'm still working a fifty-hour week, only now I'm getting paid for thirty-two hours. It's not helping me at all."

Voluntary Retirement Options

PHASED RETIREMENT. While this program is generally not considered financially advantageous for the short run, it can be effective over a period of time. Some employees who are close to retirement don't want to make the sudden break with the company, as this fictious example shows:

> Billie Gustavson worked for a research facility for thirty years. She was highly respected in the plant facilities department and throughout the organization. She was ready to make a change and to retire, but she wasn't ready to make a complete change. She had heard about a lot of people dying within two years of retirement, and she wanted to make her transition easier—and healthier. She had some projects she wanted to get involved in, but they wouldn't take her full time. So, she entered a phased retirement program. The first year, she worked three days a week; the second, two days a week. And then she retired. In the meantime, she had become actively involved in the community and was ready for the transition to a new phase of her life.

One of the considerations is retirement benefits. Can they be paid to someone who is working 60 percent time? 40 percent time? The retirement rules vary from company to company. Health benefits are also an issue.

The positive aspect of phased retirement is that the employee works closely with the organization to effect a smooth transition. The employee is happy to be productively employed and work less time, management is happy not to lose a valued person, and the remaining employees are happy with the beneficent treatment of one of their own.

The downside is that this is effective for only a small number of people and is a long-term approach to workforce reduction.

VOLUNTARY SEPARATION AND VOLUNTARY EARLY-RETIREMENT PROGRAMS. This very popular management option encourages more-expensive employees to leave the company. These programs focus their attention on employees who have been with the company for a long time and/or who have reached retirement age. Potentially exiting employees have a mixed bag of capabilities: Some "retired on the job" ten years earlier and are just waiting for a good financial excuse to leave; others are highly respected senior staff members who contribute significantly to the organization.

It is relatively easy to conduct an analysis of the number of employees who fall within a designated age and years-of-service range and to estimate the cost savings based on varying percentages of departures. For example, if 500 people with an average annual salary/benefits/overhead expense of $50,000 (a total annual wage expense of $25 million) are eligible for the early-retirement program, and 20 percent of them take advantage of the offer, the salary savings will be approximately $5 million.

Generally, early retirement candidates garner higher salaries in the company. By encouraging these long-term employees to retire or leave the company early, the company can reduce the costs of employment more rapidly and with fewer people leaving (see illustration 6). Furthermore, since they are usually in a senior staff position or are in the managerial ranks, they also create opportunities for other staff to move into the positions they have left behind. This is usually perceived to be a positive factor by both employees and managers.

The impact on the morale of the departing staff and on the remaining staff is usually positive, reflected in such statements as, "Joe was here for a long time. The company is giving him a break"; "I wanted to leave anyway"; and "Lucky Alice."

It is critical that the program be voluntary and that there be no undue pressure exerted on older employees to retire. If the program is voluntary and open to all employees who meet the requirements, there will be no discrimination issues.

Older departments may have a higher rate of leave-taking. This creates its own advantages and disadvantages. In one crafts organization, 80 percent of the supervisory staff were eligible for retirement over the ensuing five years. This sudden knowledge provided the impetus

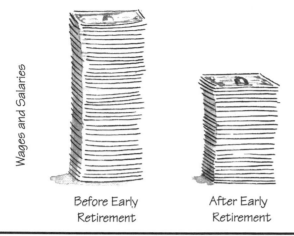

Wages and Salaries

Before Early
Retirement

After Early
Retirement

**Ilustration 6   Effect of Early Retirement on
Wage and Salary Cost to an Organization**

to start developing younger, newer employees to become the new management. But with a high rate of last-minute leave taking, there is little time to pass on the corporate culture or specially honed technical and managerial skills.

There are some major disadvantages with this program as well. The company can't easily control who leaves. Highly capable employees and managers leave, and so do the less capable. The gaps the highly competent leave behind are hard to fill, particularly if there is no groomed or obvious successor. And if there is a hiring freeze that prohibits external hiring, it's possible that the work will not get done or will be done less effectively. It takes six months to a year or longer for some departments to recover from the loss of their most valuable employees.

However, where there is a problem, there are solutions. One is to discourage highly valuable retirees from leaving by offering them more money, more flexible schedules, more perks, or temporary assignments as an incentive to stay with the organization. Another solution some companies have come up with is to invite their retirees back as consultants, temporary employees, or even short-term contract employees. Depending on the fee paid to these ex-employees, there is either very little or no overall cost savings.

Advantages to the company of hiring back one of their own retirees include:

- Choosing who they want to rehire on a part-time basis
- Reducing the cost of total salary expenditures for the part-time work
- Not having to hire behind the retiree and to pay the expense of training a new worker
- Having time to decide how to handle the workload and job functions in the future
- Continuing to receive the benefit of talented retirees' expertise

Advantages to retirees include:

- Receiving their retirement income
- Ability to act a little more independently on the job since they are employed by choice
- Having more time for transition to another external job or to change to a retirement lifestyle
- Working a reduced schedule (they don't have to fight the alarm clock every morning)
- Being paid for doing the job they were doing before

Many retirees finally leave the company within about two years' time.

Termination Options

TERMINATE FOR POOR PERFORMANCE.   Managers should terminate employees for poor performance that hasn't been improved despite all reasonable efforts at counseling, coaching, job redesign, and other similar measures. This is a belief that many workers, many managers, and many companies espouse. The difficult part is doing it. This is a short-term option if there is a performance management system in place. And that's a big *if.* It is a long-term option—two to five years or maybe never—if there is no performance management system or if it is ineffective.

The challenge of performance management systems is that they need to accurately describe an employee's job responsibilities, list the accomplishments, clearly spell out the limitations or lack of acceptable performance, and provide options for improvement. It's extraordinarily time consuming to write good performance appraisals. I remember conducting a training session in performance management to a group of field technician supervisors. They had worked with the same staff for ten to fifteen years. One of them wanted to know if he couldn't just copy last year's performance appraisal and deliver it again this year "because it hadn't changed." Sometimes poor performers have the same marginally acceptable or acceptable appraisal delivered year after year "because it just takes too long to fire a person." Employers who want to fire employees based on poor performance must be able to document it. Without the documentation, without a standardized company policy and procedure system, employers are susceptible to litigation.

The advantage of a good appraisal system is that both management and employees know where the employee stands and there are clear avenues for job improvement or justifiable dismissal. The disadvantage is that it is time consuming to establish an accurate and fair system, to train managers to implement it, and to reward or terminate employees based on their performance results.

Those who are strong advocates of appraisal systems believe that a company that has a working system in place will routinely encourage resignations or dismiss employees for whom there is a poor job fit or poor performance. Those who remain are good performers and presumably will keep the company on solid footing, which in turn will make the company less susceptible to downsizing for quality control reasons. It doesn't help in a merger or acquisition, of course, since those who are dismissed are usually the victims or losers in a buyout.

In summary, employees like to work in an environment where they know the rules and they know the rules are applied fairly. The downside to using performance appraisals to decrease the workforce is that it takes time to document and fire people for poor performance, and the numbers of actual releases is small. It is useful when it is in place and accepted by everyone and can be used in tandem with other means of workforce reduction.

RELEASE CONTRACT AND TEMPORARY WORKERS FIRST.   For years, Kelly Services, Accountemps, Adia, and other temporary employment agencies have promoted the idea of hiring highly skilled staff on a part-time or temporary basis. Their slogan is "Hire 'em when you need 'em." And for years, contract employees have worked alongside permanent staff and have done the same work with the same skill level as their company colleagues. Many like the flexibility of working at different locations with different employers or of receiving more money but fewer benefits. Some, of course, hope that the contract work is an entry into the permanent, safe, secure, regular workforce. Frequently, the casual or contract employee is the first to go when there is an imminent layoff. Occasionally, when the economy looks brighter and businesses want to hire more staff, they look first to the temporaries. (Note the new word that has been coined. We now have *temporaries* just as we have *employees*.)

There is actually a distinction in terms that needs to be described. Contract workers, or casual staff, are employees of employment agencies, job shops, or subcontracting organizations. They are paid, promoted, trained, hired, and fired by their hiring agency. The benefit to the company that uses contract staff is that they can hire or fire them based on business need and on short-term notice and without explanation. While some contract staff have been known to work for a hiring employer for years, they are still employees of the hiring agency.

By contrast, corporations will occasionally hire staff for a short-term or temporary appointment. The difference is that the workers are employees of the corporation and, based on the hiring agreement, receive the company's health and insurance benefits. Temporary employees can also be released based on business need; however, they have a little more security since many companies will wait until their contract is completed.

In the order of who gets released first, it's usually the contract staff, then the temporaries, then the regular employees. One research company no longer calls their workforce "permanent employees" since this implies a lifetime contract. Staff are regular full-time, regular part-time, or temporary employees. Hiring contracts now spell out the salary the person will earn per month but don't state how much money that is per year. Again, they don't want to imply even a year-long contract just in case they have to terminate the position.

In 1990, Charles Handy published *The Age of Unreason*, noting the rapid increase in the use of the shamrock organization, a core business surrounded by a series of companies that are contracted to perform specific work, and within each business, a small core of permanent employees surrounded and assisted by a temporary workforce.

Already the strategy at some organizations is to reduce the number of permanent employees and increase the number of casual or temporary workers. Temporary agencies are quickly adjusting their focus to "leasing employees" and providing them on a longer term basis rather than for a few weeks at a time.

TERMINATE EMPLOYEES IN JUST ONE DIVISION.   When one product line is not performing well or is no longer part of the central mission of the company, the company management may decide to eliminate the line and lay off all the line workers. The advantage to this approach is that the termination is easily explained: All employees in this one division will be released. Some might be asked to join another line, others won't. The disadvantage is that if the company wants to put employees on another experimental line or in a division with a mixed reputation, few workers will want to take the chance of being fired again. It breeds a lot of caution into employees.

TERMINATE A CONSTANT PERCENTAGE OF EMPLOYEES THROUGHOUT THE COMPANY.   While this option looks statistically sound and is considered fair and equal across the company, in practice, it has many problems. Most employees in this country, and almost all managers, consider themselves above average. In practice, whenever an across-the-board percentage cut is introduced, large numbers of managers demand exceptions for their shop "because we are special" or because they already have a shortage of employees to do the essential work. And exceptions are frequently made. Sometimes the exceptions are justified and sometimes they reek of favoritism. In order for this option to be effective, the organization needs to clearly define and explain its criteria for termination. It's an option that is widely open to charges of discrimination.

CLOSE ONE PLANT SITE.   In 1985, Caterpillar Tractor Company declared that they were closing only their San Leandro, California, plant. They kept their main plant in Illinois open. A much larger example is the Department of Defense decision in 1993 to close numerous bases throughout the United States. This is tantamount to closing multiple business sites and moving the operations lock, stock, and military personnel. The impact on the communities, the supporting businesses, and the state economy is tremendous. So is the planning for this very complex transition.

CLOSE THE BUSINESS AND TERMINATE ALL EMPLOYEES IN ALL LOCATIONS. While most business executives like to think that this is unthinkable, it does happen. A recent example is Pan Am. After selling off some equipment and valuable overseas routes and failing to negotiate a sale to a competitor, the giant airline abruptly ceased operations in December 1991.

MERGERS AND ACQUISITIONS

Love and marriage, the two go together like a horse and carriage.
—*Van Heusen-Cahn*

What does a company do with two human resources departments and two data processing units and two of this and two of that? It might have worked well on Noah's Ark, but it doesn't work well in business. Merge? Keep the best workers and the best systems and let the rest go? And who decides who will stay and who will go? When Burroughs merged with Sperry-Univac (which had previously merged with Convergent Technologies and Memorex), they called their combined firm Unisys. And the troubles continued. Since Sperry was the dominant acquiring firm, they wanted to maintain their culture, their processes, and their people. The Burroughs people began to disappear, and with every layoff more and more of them were let go. In the fall of 1990, Unisys announced that they would lay off 10,000 people nationwide— senior managers, middle managers, first-line supervisors, and rank-and-file employees. The company started its merged business with 126,000 employees. Over the last eight years, it has had fourteen to sixteen downsizings and the current workforce (1994) is around 50,000 employees. The published statement asserts these downsizings will make the company more efficient and better able to control its costs and produce a more focused and better product. Losing 60 percent of the workforce means losing good managers with experience in profitable product lines. When the new manager from the takeover company becomes the manager in the acquired company, there is the inevitable learning time required to understand the product line or function and to gain the loyalty of employees who are in a state of shock and denial.

Common options for downsizing merged companies include:

• Merging the two similar departments in the same location. Those who aren't willing to move to the new location are encouraged to leave the company, are bought out, retire, or are laid off.

- Terminating the redundant staff. The laid-off employees are usually the people from the bought-out or submerged company.

While this looks simple on paper, there are inevitable problems in the execution. Three examples come to mind:

Rolm Corporation. When computer giant IBM Corporation purchased a substantial piece of Silicon Valley darling Rolm Corporation in the 1980s, they initially had a strict hands-off policy. That policy lasted two years. IBM then increased its stake in Rolm and assigned IBM managers to key positions at Rolm. This occupation was soon followed by the imposition of the IBM culture on Rolm. Morale plummeted. Terminations grew. And finally, Rolm was sold to Siemens. Only time will tell what Rolm culture emerges.

Saga Corporation. In the 1970s this industrial food service company was flying high. It owned several restaurant chains and managed food service operations for industries, colleges, and commercial airlines. During that time it was considered to be a well-managed company with state-of-the-art business procedures. In the mid-1980s, Saga was purchased by Marriott Corporation. Marriott promptly sold off the restaurant chains and folded the industrial food services operations into its own. Saga no longer exists. The world famous art collection that once graced its headquarters now resides at nearby Stanford University.

Crocker Bank. In the mid-1980s, Wells Fargo Bank acquired San Francisco–based Crocker Bank. The bank contracted with several career transition firms to assist employees from both banks to secure appropriate employment. While the terminations and career transitions went smoothly, many of the former Crocker employees were still being referred to as "Crocker people" one or two years later.

CONCLUSION

There are a number of options for reducing the size of the workforce. Some can be used together, some are relatively simple to put in place, and there are endless variations on the basic options. The key issue is to determine the desired outcome before deciding which options to use.

Hiring Options Checklist

❏ Normal attrition
❏ Hiring options
  • Hiring slowdown
  • Hiring freeze
❏ Wage options
  • Reduce percentage of pay increases
  • Defer date of pay increases
  • Freeze wages
  • Reduce wages
  • Reduce benefits and perks

❏ Work hour options
  • Request voluntary reductions in work time
  • Offer voluntary leaves of absence without pay
  • Shut down the facility temporarily
  • Require involuntary reduction in work hours
❏ Voluntary retirement programs
  • Phased retirement
  • Voluntary separation and voluntary early-retirement programs
❏ Termination options
  • Terminate for poor performance
  • Release contract and temporary employees first
  • Terminate employees in one division or department
  • Terminate a constant percentage of employees throughout the organization
  • Close one plant site
  • Close business and terminate all employees in all locations

4

Some Legal Issues

Senior Vice President Carlos Portillo was sitting in the plush, walnut-
paneled waiting room of Harris, Goldman, and Olson, the law firm that
Streeter-Haaz frequently used for advice on employment law. Carlos was
waiting to see Marjorie Olson, one of the prominent lawyers specializing
in wrongful termination cases. Carlos was thinking back to the first time
he saw Marjorie. It was two and a half years ago, when Carlos sat in the
spectator section of a courtroom to observe the final phase of a wrongful termination suit that a former employee had brought against
Streeter-Haaz. Carlos didn't know the ex-employee, Samuel Campbell,
who was bringing the suit. Sam had been terminated four years earlier
by Carlos' predecessor.

Carlos was impressed with Marjorie's presentation. She outlined the
special steps that Streeter-Haaz had followed in handling Sam's termination: the verbal warnings and counseling, the written warnings with a
clear description of how performance must change and time lines for
changing performance, and, finally, loads of documentation. The jury
found in favor of Streeter-Haaz. Carlos had been pleased when he
returned to his office to close out the case file on Sam Campbell. The
pleasure dissipated when he totaled up what this case had cost Streeter-
Haaz: attorney fees of $23,183, court costs of $4,300, extra clerical
costs to produce and organize documents of $3,870—over $30,000—
and that didn't even count personnel time away from the job. And
Streeter-Haaz won! What would it have cost had the company lost?

That was why Carlos was anxious to see Marjorie. What could Streeter-Haaz do during this downsizing to avoid another legal situation similar to Sam Campbell's? How could they minimize the possibility of a suit?

When Carlos left Marjorie's office, he was reflecting on her advice. Marjorie's advice included three general principles:

- Do what is morally right.

- Do what is legally correct.

- Do what your written policies require.

The first principle, "Do what is morally right," was something that Carlos needed to figure out from his viewpoint and then discuss with the CEO and the executive staff. The second and third, "Do what is legally correct" and "Do what your written policies require," meant a lot of research by someone (probably Carlos) to make sure he knew what the law said, what company policies and procedures said, and that the requirements of company policies and procedures were legal.

LEGISLATION REGULATING TERMINATION AND DOWNSIZING

There are four pieces of legislature that have significant impact on termination and downsizing, and each is discussed below.

- Worker Adjustment and Retraining Notification Act (WARN)
- Age Discrimination in Employment Act (ADEA)
- Americans With Disabilities Act (ADA)
- Consolidated Omnibus Budget Reconciliation Act (COBRA)

The Internal Revenue Service's tax ruling on outplacement services is also worth noting and will be discussed briefly.

Worker Adjustment and Retraining Notification Act

The Worker Adjustment and Retraining Notification Act (WARN) was signed in early 1989 and was received with smiles by employee groups and much distrust by employer groups. As of late 1993, there appears to be little court activity generated by the legislation, perhaps because the act is serving as a deterrent to unneeded plant closings, but it is too early to tell. Another possible reason may be because there are no *real* provisions for remediation. What is clear is that managers need to know the requirements of this federal statute and to weigh them when making decisions relevant to if, when, and how to institute plant closings and mass layoffs.

While WARN is administered by the U.S. Department of Labor (DOL), only the federal courts have enforcement authority. While DOL's WARN experts will answer questions, they will not give written opinions, and their opinions and recommendations are not binding in a federal court. For these reasons, readers are strongly encouraged to obtain a copy of the WARN law and to get a legal opinion from their corporate counsel. A layperson's interpretation of the legislation is presented below.

- WARN is a federal statute and only the federal courts can enforce it.
- WARN legislation applies only to employers with 100 or more full-time employees or to employers with 100 or more full-time and part-time employees whose total work hours (not counting over-time) exceed 4,000 hours per week.
- WARN requires that covered employers planning a plant closing or mass layoff provide sixty days written notice prior to the effective date of the job loss. This written notice must be given to each affected employee (or their union, if so represented), the state dislocation worker unit, and the senior local elected public official (i.e., mayor, etc.).
- WARN defines a plant closing as involving a temporary or permanent cessation of operation at a single site for more than thirty days in which fifty or more full-time employees are affected.
- WARN defines a mass layoff as the termination of 500 or more employees or of fifty or more employees if that number is more than 33 percent of the total workforce.

For the purpose of the WARN procedures, the legislation defines job loss as a termination that is not for cause, not voluntary, and not retirement, and where the job loss exceeds six months and the work time is reduced to less than 50 percent of a normal work schedule.

The notice of a plant closing or mass layoff must relate to a specific layoff situation to meet the guidelines of WARN legislation. For instance, inserting a routine notice in each employee's pay envelope every week that says, "You are not guaranteed employment for life. If conditions change, we may have to close the plant in the next sixty days and lay you off" *does not* constitute the sixty-day notice and may be seen as an attempt to avoid the WARN requirements.

In addition to the union, the affected nonunion employees, the state dislocated worker office, and the senior local elected public official, notice must also be given to affected management, supervisory, and part-time employees (even though part-time employee numbers may not be included when calculating the total employees affected for WARN requirements).

For information on exceptions to the WARN sixty-day notice and to other provisions of the WARN legislation, readers should contact their corporate lawyer, the state dislocation worker unit, or the local Private Industry Council.

Age Discrimination in Employment Act

The Age Discrimination in Employment Act (ADEA), signed into legislation in October of 1990, is of significance to managers handling a downsizing since it imposes strict requirements on the enforceability of releases of age-discrimination claims. First of all, every effort must be made to ensure: (a) that older workers, that is, employees over age forty, have not been discriminated against in the termination decision and (b) that older workers have not been adversely impacted by how the termination decision was made.

When (a) and (b) above have been accomplished, some companies ask the affected employees to sign a release and waive their rights to sue the employer for age discrimination. Under ADEA, the release is valid only if it is "knowingly" and "voluntarily" signed. As with all legal concerns, work closely with your corporate attorneys to determine the process and the language. Even if an employee signs an ADEA release, he or she can file age discrimination charges through the EEOC, but signing the release can minimize the chances of that happening.

EARLY RETIREMENT. If an employee over age forty is being offered early retirement, it is important that specific procedures be followed. The employee should be given at least forty-five days to consider the early retirement offer and an additional seven days after signing the agreement to revoke it. To ensure that the employee understands the early retirement offer, it should include:

- The eligibility requirement
- The time lines for acceptance and implementation
- The ages and job titles of both eligible and ineligible employees

If the employee's native language is other than English, it is also a good idea to include a copy of the notification of eligibility letter in the person's language.

AMERICANS WITH DISABILITIES ACT

The Americans With Disabilities Act (ADA) was signed into law in July 1990, and it makes it illegal to discriminate in employment against qualified individuals with disabilities. It also requires that employers make "reasonable accommodation." The ADA covers all employers who employ twenty-five or more employees. After July 25, 1994, the act will cover employers with fifteen or more employees.

The ADA protects qualified individuals from discrimination. By *qualified,* it means individuals who can perform the essential job functions. To be considered disabled, individuals must have a physical or mental impairment that subsequently limits one or more major life activities. Situations that are not covered by this statute are pregnancy, obesity, sexual orientation, or active drug use. Recovering substance abusers are covered.

To ensure that the organization is in compliance with the ADA, the employer should look for and avoid (a) disparate treatment of disabled employees and (b) adverse impact on employees with disabilities.

PERSONNEL POLICIES AND LEGAL GUIDELINES

Lawsuits in general have an adverse impact on all involved. The company and its managers must spend thousands of dollars and hundreds of work hours defending their actions when these resources could be better directed toward the productivity of the company. The aggrieved employee also suffers in the legal process. The employee must direct his or her energy away from the job search process and often gets bogged down in a negative no-win battle with the employer. The only ones who really win are the attorneys who derive fees from the process. We recommend adapting the following procedures for personnel policies and legal guidelines.

- Look at the organization's affirmative action plan to ensure that it is current and up to date. Then be sure that the proposed action conforms to the plan.

- Follow the organization's published policies and procedures. Don't make employment or termination decisions that can't be justified. Don't make termination decisions without sufficient documentation.

- If there is a deviation from the published policies and procedures, be sure that it is to give the employee in a protected class more.

- Look through the personnel files on all affected employees, especially senior managers and executives, to ensure that there are no special contracts or promises for which the company can now be held liable.

- If exiting employees are asked to sign a waiver, the employee must know and understand what he or she is signing. Use clear and simple language; give the employee sufficient time to decide to sign or not; encourage the employee to have the agreement reviewed by a lawyer.

- When offering an employee a severance package, seriously consider offering salary continuation rather than payment of one lump sum. The probability of employees suing the organization while they are still receiving a check each payday is very low.

- Give as much notice as possible. Lawyers will generally advise organizations to do this since it will reduce exposure to a lawsuit. However, managers as a group oppose too much notice. They fear that the morale of the survivors will suffer and that the employees might sabotage the plant. There is no evidence to support this fear. In general, employees appreciate the advance notice and work to support the action if the communication is clear and forthright. Managers also think that offering a waiver to the exiting employee for his or her signature could create problems. For instance, the employee might get the idea to file a lawsuit or complaint, even though it is without merit. Employees, however, generally respect a legal document. If they are inclined to sue, they will have already had that idea in mind.

COBRA

Finally, it is appropriate to review the COBRA legislation. The Consolidated Omnibus Budget Reconciliation Act was passed into law in 1985 (P.L. 99-272 April 7, 1986) and affects employers with twenty or more employees. COBRA benefits should not be tied to the signing of a waiver—they are due the employee by law. Peter S. Wantuch, Principal of PSW Benefit Resources in Burlingame, California, who consults with companies concerning COBRA and other employee benefits, recommends the following written materials for his clients.

Sample general announcement letter. The general announcement letter (see figure 1) is to be given to each employee and his or her eligible enrolled dependents at the time of initial benefit election. This form informs the new employee and his or her eligible enrolled dependents of their rights under COBRA.

Employer notification to qualified beneficiaries. The employer notification to qualified beneficiaries (see figure 2) is to be individualized and is to be delivered to each employee at the time of the qualified event. This form should also be sent to the best known address of each enrolled qualified beneficiary. It informs the qualified beneficiaries of the cost of each benefit he or she may continue, as well as the date that current coverage will terminate, should COBRA not be elected. It also informs each qualified beneficiary of the maximum duration of COBRA coverage, should it be elected.

Spousal information for COBRA. The spousal information for the COBRA form (see figure 3) is to be sent to the best known address for a spouse that will lose coverage due to a qualifying event. It informs the spouse of his or her rights under COBRA.

Written request for continued health coverage. The written request for continued health care coverage (see figure 4) is to be given to all qualified beneficiaries at the time of the qualifying event. It is the vehicle used by the qualified beneficiary to let the employer know of his or her planned elections.

This information is presented only as guidance for forms to use in an organization's COBRA administration program. The exact contents will vary according to each organization's benefits programs that are subject to COBRA continuation, as well as the administrative arrangements established by the organization.

Notice of Continuation of Group Health Coverage Rights

This notice is intended to inform you, in a summary fashion, of your and your covered dependents' rights and obligations under the continuation coverage provisions of the Federal COBRA Act of 1985. You, your spouse, and any other qualified family members should take the time to read this summary notice carefully.

If you are an employee covered by *[Name of insurance carrier]*, hereafter referred to as "the Plan," you have a right to elect continuation coverage if you lost your group health coverage because of the termination of your employment (for reasons other than gross misconduct on your part) or a reduction in hours of employment.

If you are the covered spouse of an employee covered by the Plan, you have the right to elect continuation coverage for yourself if you lose group health coverage under the Plan for any of the following reasons:

a. The death of your spouse

b. A termination of your spouse's employment (for reasons other than gross misconduct) or reduction in your spouse's hours of employment

c. The divorce or legal separation from your spouse

d. The Plan provides loss of coverage due to entitlement to Medicare

In the case of a covered dependent child of an employee covered by the Plan, such child has the right to continue coverage if group health coverage under the Plan is lost for any of the following reasons:

a. The death of a parent

b. The termination of a parent's employment (for reasons other than gross misconduct) or reduction in a parent's hours of employment

c. The parent's divorce or legal separation

d. The Plan provides loss of coverage due to entitlement to Medicare

e. The dependent ceases to be a "dependent child" under the Plan

Continuation coverage may also apply to covered retirees and their covered dependents in the event the employer files a Title 11 bankruptcy. Special rules may apply for this event. Please contact the Plan administrator for additional information.

Figure 1   Sample General Announcement Letter

Used by permission of Peter S. Wantuck, PSW Benefit Resources, Burlingame, CA.

You or a covered dependent have the responsibility to inform the Plan administrator within 60 days of a divorce, legal separation, or a child losing dependent status under the Plan. The employer has the responsibility to notify the Plan administrator of the employee's death, termination of employment, or reduction in hours resulting in the loss of group health coverage.

When the Plan administrator is notified that one of these events has happened, the Plan administrator will, in turn, notify you that you have the right to elect continuation coverage. You have 60 days from the date you would lose coverage, because of one of the events described above, to inform the Plan administrator that you want continuation coverage.

If you do not elect continuation coverage, your group health coverage will end [the last day of the month following termination] or [the last day of active employment].

If you elect continuation coverage, the employer is required to give you group health coverage which, as of the time coverage is being continued, is identical to the coverage provided under the Plan to similarly situated active employees and dependents. If, however, the group coverage changes, your COBRA continuation coverage will also change.

You may maintain continuation coverage for 36 months unless you lost group health coverage because of a termination of employment or reduction in hours. In those cases, the continuation coverage period is 18 months. This 18 months may be extended to a maximum of 36 months if other events (such as a death or divorce) occur during the 18-month period. If you are totally disabled, for Social Security purposes, on the date of the termination of employment, you may be entitled to 11 additional months (for a total of 29 months) of continuation coverage at an increased premium rate which will equal 150% of the normal group rate. The totally disabled person must inform the Plan administrator of the Social Security determination of disability within 60 days of that determination. Also, if a covered employee becomes entitled to Medicare, his or her dependent covered under the group health Plan is entitled to continuation coverage for 36 months. However, continuation coverage will end for any of the following reasons:

a. The employer no longer provides group health coverage for any of its employees

b. You (or your dependents) fail to make the appropriate payment for continuation coverage

Figure 1   Sample General Announcement Letter (continued)

c. You (or your dependents) are covered under another group health plan that does not contain a preexisting condition exclusion or limitation which affects you (or dependents)

d. You (or your dependents) are entitled to Medicare

You do not have to submit written evidence of good health to elect continuation coverage.

You will have to make all of the payments for your continuation coverage unless the employer or Plan sponsor specifically tells you otherwise in writing. You will have 45 days from the date of your election to make the initial payment; however, continuation coverage will not become effective until the full and correct payment is made and received. You will have a grace period of 30 days in which to make all other regularly scheduled premium payments. The Plan administrator may charge a 2% administrative fee each month based on the premium. Also, your premium will rise if the employer's premium rises.

At the end of the respective 18-month, 29-month, or 36-month continuation coverage period, you will be allowed to enroll in an individual conversion health plan then being offered in most states.

If you have any questions about your rights and obligations under COBRA continuation of health care benefits, please contact the Plan administrator.

Plan Administrator:
Telephone Number:
Address:

Also, if you have a change in marital status, or you or your spouse have changed addresses, please notify the Plan administrator.

For more and complete details, please refer to the COBRA Act of 1985 [P.L. 99-272 April 7, 1986]

Figure 1   Sample General Announcement Letter (continued)

Memorandum

To: [Employee (and spouse and dependents, if applicable)]
From:
Subject: Notice of Right to Continue Coverage Under the COBRA
          Act of 1985

Date:

Your medical and dental coverage (and that of your spouse and dependents, if applicable), under the group insurance plan terminates on
_____.

If you are not covered under any other group health care plan, or have a
preexisting condition that is excluded by another group health care plan,
you may continue coverage without interruption for a specified time. You
also have the right to continue any fringe benefit plan(s) in which you
participate. Please see the section entitled "When Continued Coverage
Ceases" for a description of how long and under what circumstances
your COBRA continuation coverage may continue.

Cost of Continued Coverage

As an employee of _____,
you and your eligible dependents who have elected coverage are covered
under the medical and dental insurance plans *[until the end of the month*
in which you terminate employment] or *[through your last day as an*
active employee].

The total monthly cost to you for your current medical and dental plans,
if you select coverage under COBRA, will be as follows:

Plan	Self cost	Dependent cost	Total
Medical			
Dental			

Please note that if our group coverage changes, your coverage will also
change.

Elected coverage must be continuous from the date your employer-paid
coverage ceases on _____. Payments are due the
first of the month for coverage to be continued for the subsequent month.
Failure to pay this amount within 30 days of the due date will result in loss
of coverage without the opportunity for reinstatement. (We may charge
an additional 2% to cover our administrative costs.)

Figure 2   Employer Notification to Qualified Beneficiaries

Used by permission of Peter S. Wantuck, PSW Benefit Resources, Burlingame, CA.

Rates will be adjusted based on changes in the regular group rates. You will be notified of any rate changes prior to the date your payment is due.

When Continued Coverage Ceases

The continued coverage will cease for any person upon the earliest of the following:

a. 18 months if the qualifying event is termination of employment or reduction in work hours

b. 29 months from the date continuation began for individuals whose coverage was extended due to total disability commencing on or before the time of the COBRA qualifying event

c. 36 months for all other qualifying events

d. The date the employer ceases to provide any group health plan to employees

e. The date upon which coverage ceases because of failure to pay the premium (including any administrative charge) on a timely basis as previously noted

f. The date on which the qualified beneficiary first becomes eligible under another group plan as an employee or becomes eligible for Medicare, except if the individual has a preexisting condition that is limited or excluded by such plan

g. In the case of a qualified beneficiary who is a spouse, the date on which remarriage coverage under another group plan occurs, except if the individual has a preexisting condition that is limited or excluded by such plan

Conversion Rights

Once continuation coverage ceases for any person, that person may obtain a conversion health care policy then in existence without evidence of insurability, as provided under the terms of the Plan. You will have the right to apply for this conversion plan within 31 days of the end of the COBRA coverage.

How to Elect Continued Coverage

Complete the attached form and return it *within 60 days* of the date group coverage ceases, or within 60 days of the date of this notice. If the appropriate payment is not received within 45 days of your election to continue coverage, you will lose your right to continuation coverage. The form and appropriate payment should be mailed to:

Figure 2   Employer Notification to Qualified Beneficiaries (continued)

Spousal Information for COBRA Act of 1985

During the time your spouse was employed at *[Name of Employer]*, he or she enrolled you and/or members of your family in the group insurance plan, which offered health benefits. As the spouse of a former employee, you have the right to elect COBRA coverage for yourself and your dependent children. The information contained in this packet is extremely important; we advise you to read it carefully.

The following paragraphs contain information you should know in order to make a decision regarding the continuation of your health insurance plan.

Who can elect COBRA coverage?

You, as the spouse of a former employee, can elect coverage for yourself and the members of your family who have Plan coverage on the last day of your spouse's employment. You cannot, however, decline coverage for your spouse.

What COBRA coverage can I elect?

You may elect any benefits that your spouse elected for you, and that were in place on the last day of your spouse's employment while you were covered under the group insurance plan(s).

How long do I have to make up my mind?

You have 60 days from the Plan termination date on the memorandum to make up your mind.

When is my first payment due?

If necessary, you have 45 days (*after the 60 days* noted above) to make your first payment. You must, however, remit the total premium due as of the last day of coverage under the group plan.

When are my second and subsequent payments due?

Each premium payment is due on the first of the month. Failure to pay this amount within 30 days of the due date will result in loss of coverage without the opportunity of reinstatement of COBRA coverage.

Figure 3   Spousal Information for COBRA

What must I do?

Carefully read the COBRA information that you have received. The first section is an explanation of your rights. The second part is a memorandum that explains when your Plan will begin and the costs involved for the coverage that your spouse selected for you while he or she was an employee at *[Name of Employer]*.

The third section contains the qualifying information and the signature that is necessary in order for you to elect continued health coverage under COBRA.

How do I elect COBRA coverage?

After you have read the information contained in this packet and have decided that you want COBRA coverage, please look at the third section, "Written Request for Continued Health Coverage Under the COBRA Act of 1985," and complete all of the requested information. Be sure to sign your name and date the document. Send the form to the address below.

If you decide that you **do not want** COBRA coverage (you cannot decline coverage for your spouse), please complete section 3 under "Written Request for Continued Health Coverage Under the COBRA Act of 1985"; sign your name; date the document; and return it to:

Note: Failure to return the completed COBRA election form within the required time frame will be assumed to be a declination of coverage.

Figure 3   Spousal Information for COBRA (continued)

**Written Request for Continued Health Coverage
Under the COBRA Act of 1985**

(Please type or print clearly)

1. Name of Employee   Date of Birth   Social Security Number

   _____   ___ / ___ / ___   _____ / ___ / _____

2. Name and Address (of person requesting continuation of
   coverage)

   Name _____

   Street/Apt. # _____

   City/State _____   Zip _____

   Date of Birth _____   SS# _____

   a. Relationship to Employee: _____
                                       Self/Spouse/Dependent

   b. Qualifying Event (please check one):
      ❏ Termination of employment
      ❏ Reduction in hours
      ❏ Divorce/separation
      ❏ Death
      ❏ Entitlement to Medicare
      ❏ Child ceases to qualify as a covered dependent
      ❏ Other:

   c. Date of Qualifying Event: _____

3. Election (please check):   Coverage:
                                          Medical   Medical &
                                           Only   Dental
   ❏ I do not elect to continue coverage.   _____   _____
   ❏ I elect to continue coverage for
      myself only.   _____   _____

Figure 4   Written Request for Continued Health Coverage

Used by permission of Peter S. Wantuck, PSW Benefit Resources, Burlingame, CA.

	Coverage:	
	Medical Only	Medical & Dental

❑ I elect to continue coverage for myself and my eligible dependents listed below   _____   _____

❑ I elect to continue coverage for my eligible dependents, only, as listed below   _____   _____

Dependent Name	Date of Birth	Relationship to Employee	SS#
_____	___/___/___	_____	___/___/___
_____	___/___/___	_____	___/___/___
_____	___/___/___	_____	___/___/___

4. I agree to submit monthly payments in the amount(s) below, which are due on the first day of the month beginning on _____ .

Failure to pay these amounts(s) within 30 days of the due date will result in the loss of coverage without the opportunity of reinstatement.

Qualified Beneficiaries: **Monthly Premium(s):**

Covered employee only $ _____

Spouse or ex-spouse $ _____

Dependent child only $ _____

Covered employee and spouse $ _____

Covered employee and
     one dependent child* $ _____

Spouse or ex-spouse and
     one dependent child* $ _____

Covered employee, spouse, and
     one dependent child $ _____

*Add $ _____ for each additional child.

Figure 4   Written Request for Continued Health Coverage (continued)

These forms must be revised for any employer who offers any of the following benefits/plan designs:

- Groups that offer medical flexible spending accounts (FSAs)
- Multiemployer plans
- Groups that offer coverage to retirees
- Groups that offer employee assistance programs (EAPs) that are more than "referral-only" type plans

These materials should not be constructed as legal advice pertaining to any factual situation; legal and tax advisors must be consulted to ensure compliance.

IRS Tax Rulings on the Value of Outplacement and Career Transition Services

One of the more controversial issues is the desire of some companies and some individuals to negotiate to receive a fixed dollar amount in lieu of transition services. The Outplacement Industry Tax Coalition (OITC) published the following statement in its *Tax Bulletin* of August 21, 1992:

> The Internal Revenue Service issued Revenue Ruling 92-69 (August 20, 1992) excluding employer paid outplacement services from the W-2 compensation of recipients of the service. The ruling recognized the substantial business benefit to an employer of providing outplacement services (such as promoting a positive corporate image, sustaining employee morale, and avoiding wrongful termination suits) that is distinct from the benefit than an employer would derive from the mere payment of additional compensation. (p.1)

The twelve-page IRS document describes three examples:

- Employer-provided outplacement services when there is a reduction in workforce
- Employer-provided outplacement services during annual company turnovers
- Cash options in lieu of outplacement services

After reviewing the law and presenting their analysis, the IRS concluded that outplacement services as described in the first two examples may be excluded from gross income as tax-free working condition fringe benefits under Internal Revenue Code Section 132 (d).

When an employee has an option to receive a cash severance payment in lieu of outplacement, the value of the outplacement received is taxable to the extent the severance payment is reduced. In the example cited in the ruling, the employee could deduct this amount as a miscellaneous itemized deduction on the employee's federal income tax return.

The ruling ends by stating that an individual could continue to receive outplacement without taxation even though the employee is no longer currently employed by the employer. The IRS Revenue Ruling appears in the September 8, 1992 issue of the *IRS Bulletin*, 1992-36.

CONCLUSION

Legal actions require the services of legal professionals. Employees want assurance that they are not being unfairly treated, and they want assurance that their legal rights are not being violated. Lawyers have a bag of stories about managers and companies who act impulsively when they decide to terminate an individual or a group of people and about the years and money it takes to clean up the mess. The advice given at the beginning of this chapter still holds:

- Do what is morally right.
- Do what is legally correct.
- Do what your written policies require.

5

Preparing Management for Downsizing

Louise Rodriguez had been with Streeter-Haaz for fifteen years. She had worked her way up from a clerical position to her current job as quality assurance manager for the SK and MK lines. She worked long hours and prided herself on being an excellent manager. Streeter-Haaz recognized her productivity and loyalty through regular promotions and pay raises.

The company sent her annually to the best quality assurance seminars available, even when it meant flying her across the country to do so. That afternoon Louise arrived at corporate headquarters for a management training session in the president's conference room. Four o'clock in the afternoon was a strange time for a training session, she thought. And the president's office was a strange place to hold it. The president's assistant had called that morning to notify Louise of the training session and to ensure that she would be there.

As Louise took her seat at the almost full conference table, she glanced at the packet of materials waiting for her. The cover page read "Terminating Employees: Some Helpful Hints for Managers." She read it again to make sure she was reading it correctly. She was stunned. What was happening? Who was being terminated? What in the world could a manager do to make terminating someone less stressful?

THE ROLE OF MANAGEMENT

Each level of management has a significant role to play in successfully managing the downsizing process and outcome. To play that role, each person at each level needs to understand what is expected of them. The board of directors, the CEO, senior managers, and the firing managers each have a unique message to deliver to a variety of constituencies. What they say and do in the initial stages of the actual downsizing will significantly affect the organization over the first month or two as well as for the long term.

This section serves as a briefing chapter for the board of directors, CEO, the senior managers, the firing managers, and their advisors.

Board of Directors

The role of the board of directors is to ensure that there is a business plan in place so that the organization can endure and prosper. The issues that the board needs to address include:

- Is this a change or a shift in direction?
- Do we have the resources—technical and managerial, dollars and time—to achieve our business goals?
- Are we maintaining the credibility of the major stakeholders—the financial community, suppliers, customers, and employees?

One of the major roles of the board of directors is to review the overall plan to ensure that the best possible practices are being used to support the downsizing effort. When there is a rich diversity in board membership, the company is more likely to receive recommendations on the best practices for downsizing.

The Chief Executive Officer (CEO)

The CEO is the architect of the organization. He or she provides vital leadership to relate to a number of audiences the big picture of the company's economic and financial conditions, plans for the future, market and customer needs, and current actions necessary to achieve corporate goals. This message is delivered to the company's managers, employees, the press, the business community at large, and the shareholders. While his or her appearances and public remarks may be brief, they are critical for setting the tone for what can become either a morale and public relations fiasco or an exercise in competent leadership.

Senior Managers

The senior managers are the engineers who build to the architect's design and specifications. In a downsizing effort, they reconstruct the company to meet the CEO's new organizational vision. While both the CEO and the senior managers have unique primary responsibilities, they need to work together to achieve the overall objective. Various internal and external resources are available to help them achieve their specific roles.

CONSULTING RESOURCES

In preparing for the public declaration of the downsizing, the CEO and senior managers have a number of consulting resources who can assist with the sequence of actions and the positioning of statements. While the CEO is knowledgeable about the company's current business condition and desired future situation, the probability is high that others will have useful suggestions for how to effectively state the company's plans to others. Some examples of consultants include the following:

An internal senior organizational development consultant. An organizational development consultant usually has ready access to the CEO and other senior executives and generally has expertise in transition strategies, long-range planning, organizational politics, and savvy on the impact of senior management's actions on the organization and the external environment.

A public relations manager. This person can not only lay out a strategy and time schedule to coordinate the written, verbal, and personal interactions of the CEO and senior managers but can also schedule photo opportunities and produce much of the material. If there will be contact with radio, television, the newspapers, or talk shows, it is essential that the executive officers be well versed in how to manage their comments. Briefings and in-house trial runs will increase the chances of getting the company's message accurately conveyed to the employees, stockholders, and press. If managers don't have a well-thought-out, prepared statement, the press will come to their own conclusions and report them as fact.

An external management consultant. This may be someone who is a principal of the career transition or organizational development firm that the organization is using. The CEO uses the consultant as a sounding board for ideas and strategies and for releasing his or her feelings in a confidential environment. The external consultant generally has a lot of practical experience in the termination process and can indicate just what is likely to happen and what is unlikely. CEOs are rarely neutral about the prospect of downsizing their company; they, too, are angry, morose, or agitated about their failure. It is, after all, their company and their very public statement about their competency to lead the organization into a new direction. Thus, even though the CEO publicly expresses his or her feelings about the downsizing, there is still a public face that is more contained than the private pain. It is very useful for a CEO to have someone to whom that pain can be expressed.

As the architect of the downsizing, the CEO communicates first with the board of directors, and then with the managers, employees, press, business community at large, and shareholders.

COMMUNICATING TO IMPORTANT GROUPS

There are seven groups that the CEO must communicate effectively with in order to successfully move through the crisis of downsizing. Swift and competent consulting and practice briefings for the chief executive officer are critical for success. Either internal or external consultants are ideal people to coach the CEO.

Board of Directors

Directors are often opinion leaders in different sectors of the business community. It is particularly important at this time for the CEO to ensure as much two-way communication as possible with the board. It is common for the CEO to start by briefing the board on both the immediate and long-term impact of the current economic condition or the "health" of the company. Just as important is that board members have the opportunity to voice concerns and opinions about the impending downsizing, and that this discussion be given adequate time to allow the ventilation of fear by individual board members. In many cases, the board member will be voicing an opinion held by other members of his or her community. This is an excellent time for the CEO to look to the board for constructive advice and counsel.

Managers

Managers look to the company's top leadership for signs of what is to come and offer suggestions and recommendations. If the leaders— the CEO and executive officers—exhibit clarity of purpose and the determination to succeed, are credible, and have understanding and compassion for the employees, then the managers will view the current downsizing situation as a challenge to be squarely addressed and overcome. If the leader fails to convey a clear vision (even if he or she has a clear vision), lacks foresight in the eyes of employees, or appears psychologically remote from the impact of the downsizing on staff, then the managers will be drawn into a downward spiral of low morale and decreasing productivity. To the managers, the CEO can be a true barometer of corporate morale.

Employees

In U.S. corporations, the CEO can be very much a parental figure to rank-and-file employees. Most employees spend more waking hours each workweek with their co-workers than they do with family members. With the advent of electronic mail (E-mail), many CEOs have the opportunity to route personalized memos directly to any employee's personal computer system.

Figure 5 shows a sample memo that the CEO might send to each employee. In some companies, this can be done by E-mail, which is instantaneous and gives the recipient the impression that it was personally directed to him or her by the CEO.

This type of memo can let the employees know of all of the activities that have been undertaken to avoid layoffs. Note that the CEO should never put anything into a memo that he or she would not want

STREETER-HAAZ CORPORATION

From: Stuart Aubret, President and CEO

To: All employees

Date: February 19, 1994

Subject: State of our corporate health

As many of you are aware, the recent economic downturn has resulted in a significant decline in orders for the SK-2000 and, to a lesser extent, the related MK series products. In an effort to bridge this problem, you have responded well by cooperating with our cost-cutting procedures:

- We reduced capital expenditures by 63 percent.

- We curtailed noncritical travel.

- We postponed off-site training until next fiscal year.

- We froze 95 percent of all new hire requisitions.

In spite of these unselfish efforts by all employees, we have found it necessary to take further actions.

- Effective February 20, all senior managers (directors and vice presidents) have volunteered to take a 5 percent salary reduction.

- Effective February 20, my direct reports (senior vice presidents) and I will take a 7 percent salary reduction.

I want each of you to know my personal commitment to navigate this crisis with minimal impact on all of you. I will continue to use this means to keep you posted on our situation. Thank you for your loyalty and support.

Figure 5   Sample Corporate Communication

to see on the front page of the local newspaper. Leaks *always* occur. In addition, the memo should tell the truth. If layoffs are planned, don't say that they're not.

No matter how brief, one of the most important functions of the CEO is to personally talk with individuals or groups of employees at all—or most—company locations. During normal times, the CEO's talk may involve kicking off the companywide meeting with a state-of-the-company presentation. During the downsizing, the CEO is the appropriate person to launch the companywide employee conference with a state-of-the-crisis presentation of the business imperatives, steps for remediation, and desired end result. The CEO can then turn the microphone over to those who are responsible for the downsizing and career transition activities, such as the human resources manager, who can talk about severance pay, benefits, and the job search assistance available for affected employees. The CEO's messages to employees should include:

- The company response to market, customer, and competitive forces
- A statement of what is actually happening in the company and to specific products
- Actions the company has taken to increase competitiveness and productivity
- Alternatives implemented prior to selecting downsizing
- The CEO's personal feelings about the downsizing
- Actions the company will take to facilitate the transition for employees
- The future direction the company will take and actions that will be taken to support it (this is primarily for the benefit of those employees who form the ongoing strategic workforce)

Meanwhile, several months later... Stuart Aubret took the microphone at a specially called companywide meeting: "As you are aware, orders for our SK model are down this year by more than 35 percent. This has not changed for two quarters. We have tightened engineering and manufacturing. We have frozen new hiring. We have curtailed nonessential travel. We have reduced the size of our raw material inventory. We have instituted paycuts for senior managers and executives. These measures have reduced our losses, but not enough. Based on market forecasts and consultations with my staff, I have made the difficult and painful decision to reduce and eliminate our ongoing losses by closing the SK production line. This will make available resources to improve the competitiveness of our remaining businesses. But it also means laying off 176 workers effective at the end of this month. We have tried other measures that didn't work. We are without an alternative. This is a painful recourse, but a necessary one for the survival of the company. The company will be expanding its MK line and will seek other product lines in keeping with our customer demands. I look forward to working with those of you who will be part of our ongoing strategic workforce. I also look forward to supporting the efforts of those progressing their careers to jobs with other organizations. For those of you who are part of the SK line, let me turn the podium over to Christina Perugia, the head of our human resources department, who can fill you in on the specifics of the career transition assistance that we are providing for these 176 workers."

Media

The business media reports on the actions of companies and the statements of the company's business leaders and employees. Six- to ten-second "sound bites" of information are usually all that will be shown on the evening television news. One- to six-inch stories of facts and public rumors are all that will be printed in the newspapers. If a downsizing is particularly large or messy, it will get larger coverage. The reputation of the company can be drawn through the mud in the business pages or the front pages of the local newspaper by a combination of publicized rumors and official corporate silence. There is nothing worse than the radio or television news anchor describing the rumors about an impending layoff at a corporation and announcing that "the president's office is not returning any of our calls."

Rumors of downsizing can be ugly. For example, it was rumored that a high-profile computer maker was expected to lay off some 900 employees over the subsequent two weeks. The press had interviewed employees in the parking lot about their feelings. Employees were in the dark; they didn't know what was going to happen. Many criticized top management for their well-publicized seven-figure salaries— especially the million dollar bonus given to the CEO. On Monday of that week, a few dozen employees held a rally to voice displeasure about the rumor that lower level employees would suffer the brunt of the downsizing and that top executives would still be getting their generous salaries and perks. This rally was reported on the front page of the local newspaper and covered by the local evening TV news. Thursday, when the company finally passed out the pink slips to the 900 affected employees, they also announced that the CEO and other top managers would take an immediate 15 percent pay cut and bonuses would be eliminated. While the executive pay cut was an excellent gesture, it was seen by employees, and more importantly, by the general public, as anticlimactic. Just think about the great public relations mileage the company could have gotten had the announcement of the executive pay cut been announced just one week earlier. The television, radio, and newspaper coverage would have focused on the "leadership and sacrifice" of the executives instead of their implied indifference to the bleak economic future of their 900 employees. Consider the amount of damage control that a very brief (10 to 15 seconds long) but sincere, substantive, and credible announcement from the CEO could have generated.

Stuart Aubret was ready to make his announcement to the press: "The Streeter-Haaz corporation has suffered *(note the use of a feeling word)* a year-long decline in the sales of its major product line *(identifies the business cause over a period of time and tells people that this is not an instant reaction to a short-term event)*. Other companies within the industry have downsized prior to us. We have held off for as long as we could. The federal government has continued to allow dumping of products by foreign nations *(spreads the blame to the responsible parties and lets people know that there wasn't any other choice)*. Reluctantly, the executives and board of directors have decided *(identifies who has made the decision)* to close the SK production line, which will affect 176 workers *(identifies which specific work groups and the numbers of employees affected)*. We are working closely with our employees to help them make the transition into new positions *(shows concern for the people)*. The people we are letting go are a lot better prepared to compete in the marketplace because of the training and skill development they received while they were with us *(states that people are better for having worked for the organization and that their people are treated well and are an asset to the community)*. We will continue to develop our other profitable production lines *(indicates a future direction)*."

A written press release also needs to be available and given to local newspapers and radio and television stations. (See also the section "Announcing the Downsizing to the Outside World" in chapter 10. A further note: Before talking with the media or the public, it is essential to formulate a sound bite phrase that shows caring for the employees, the community, those displaced, and the economic viability of the company. And then repeat the phrase again and again.

Business Community

An organization's image in the business community can be critical. Company credibility with customers, suppliers, and even by its competitors is important. When granting credit or considering purchasing and employment actions, most decision makers will turn to a business colleague and ask, "What do you know about Streeter-Haaz Corporation? How are they viewed in the business community?"

I can recall a conversation with a headhunter about whether to advise a colleague to apply for a job at a defense contractor. The headhunter's response was, "Make sure your friend gets combat pay. That company is known to chew people up and spit them out." When I spoke with a human resources manager at the company in question, she confirmed that they now had to pay about 20 percent over market to attract and retain qualified professional employees.

In preparing messages for the business community, make sure that you present the following:

- Desired corporate image
- Vision of the future business
- Actions that are being taken to achieve the vision
- Strength of the workforce that will achieve the goals
- Teamwork required to support those displaced as well as the future of the company

Shareholders

Shareholders are in a unique and interesting position. As economic stakeholders, they have a bottom-line concern for profit and the continued viability of the organization and for the management's ability to tactically achieve short-term and strategic long-range planning. As human beings who identify with the management of the organization, they often have a genuine compassion and concern for the company's employees. Just imagine yourself as the well-paid CEO presiding over a shareholder's meeting and being confronted by irate stockholders asking questions such as these:

- "How can you lay off all of these low paid clerks and assemblers, many of whom are single parents, when you gave yourself a 10 percent raise over your already inflated salary?"
- "Why are you spending so much money on career transition services when it could go into advertising and increasing profits?"
- "What are you doing to take this company into increased profitability?"

Preparing for anticipated questions by distributing a handout of commonly asked questions and answers about a planned downsizing eases the confrontation. The CEO should comment that the questions and answers have also been shared with the local community, civic leaders, and the media. Note that such shareholder meetings are also open to the media.

Employees' Families

It is not only in Japan that the family is part of the company. In many small, medium, and even large companies, the career is a family affair. The company sponsors barbecues and ball games and encourages involvement by all family members. In these cases, it is very appropriate for the CEO to address groups of family members. While similar to the presentations to employees, this presentation should be more personal, and the CEO should spend as much time as possible describing the support systems and answering the questions and concerns of family members. Here are some questions that might be posed to the CEO:

- "What about our insurance coverage? We can't afford private medical insurance for John, myself, and our five kids."

- "How long will Pat's unemployment benefits last?"
- "Will you be rehiring next year when the economy improves?"
- "How come there is no seniority list for rehiring? My wife has been with this company for over twenty years, and she should have priority for rehire."
- "Why are you still posting job vacancies while you're downsizing?"

Checklist for CEO Communications

❏ Resources
- Board of directors
- Executive officers
- Internal organizational development professionals
- External management consultants
- Public relations

❏ Communicate to
- Board of directors
- Managers
- Employees
- Media
- Business community
- Shareholders
- Employees' families (if appropriate)

PREPARING MIDDLE MANAGERS

The department manager is often responsible for a specific group of people who work and relate with each other on a daily basis. They often socialize together and are frequently described as a family. The department manager is the head of the family unit. This person has a very tough job. He or she must relate how business decisions made in a remote headquarters will affect the very real people that the department manager sees and talks with every day. The department manager's discussions will be in two phases. The first will be during the time that the supervisors and managers of those affected will be told of the downsizing; the second will occur immediately after the terminations are announced and the survivors gather in stunned silence to hear the official news. In both cases, it will be important to explain the following points in simple, nontechnical terms:

- The business and economic problems that have precipitated the situation
- What other cost reduction measures were instituted or considered and why
- How other departments are affected in relation to this department
- Who specifically is being affected
- What functions and responsibilities will be changed

Inevitably, there are some difficult questions that someone in the group will ask:

- "After this downsizing, are there any other downsizings planned?" The answers are "Yes," "No," or "I don't know." It is important to be honest. If the answer is unknown, don't be afraid to say so.
- "What will be done for the affected employees?" The corporate policy on layoffs and severance pay should be summarized and described and related directly to the specific benefits and services being given to the affected employees.
- "Will employees be eligible for recall? Will they have bumping rights? What specific job-search assistance will they be given?" The corporate policy should be repeated, even if it was stated five minutes before (the answer is important to the person who asked the question). The job search assistance that employees are receiving should be described in detail. Written handouts describing the layoff/termination and the services provided to former employees should also be distributed.
- "What will happen to me? to my job? Am I the next to go?" Truthfulness is essential. Again, if the manager doesn't know, say so. If the ongoing strategic workforce is to become productive again quickly, the trust level between management and all levels of employees must be evident. The consequences of not being straightforward are that employees spend more time tuning into the grapevine and more time worrying about their own job future than doing their job. Sun Microsystems announced to one division of their operation that the function was going to be outsourced and they would be laid off in four to twelve months. They provided career development workshops for everyone in the division and kept them informed about decisions as they were made. It was a surprise to everyone that productivity went up.

The department manager has another task: to make an initial appearance in the survivor training session scheduled for all remaining employees on the next day. After the survivor training, the department manager should assume a highly visible profile, conversing with the strategic workforce managers and employees, answering their questions, and short-circuiting potential negative rumors. This is particularly true with the department manager's direct reports, usually managers and supervisors themselves. To these managers and supervisors, the department manager is their only direct link to headquarters, to the place where job decisions are made. After the crisis of a downsizing, everyone up and down the chain of command needs frequent reassurance that all those who have been released have been notified.

PREPARING THE FIRING MANAGER

The firing manager is probably the most uncomfortable player in the termination arena. Many career transition counselors will testify to the guilt, discomfort, and depression that firing managers have reported. Usually, the actual termination is extraordinarily painful for the firing manager who has spent several days or weeks selecting which employees will be dismissed and then preparing to deliver the difficult message that will affect his or her employees.

The person who delivers the termination message to the employee is usually the immediate or direct supervisor. In reality, many supervisors try to avoid conducting the termination. A favorite ploy is to schedule out-of-town travel during the week of the planned termination and to delegate the chore to a "Mr. Roberts" type who can relate well to the soon-to be-displaced employee.

Not every CEO has a "Mr. Roberts" available, but many will want to delegate the task to the human resource department. The manager's excuse is that HR is the people department and they know all the rules and know how to fire people better. The reality is that the line organization has prime responsibility for its people: They hire them, manage them, train them, and, if necessary, terminate them. Human Resources is a support department to the line organization whose role is to assist line management in meeting the needs of the organization, including advising them on how to most successfully effect a downsizing. One more word about the consequences of delegating the termination notification to human resources: If HR does the firing, the remaining core workforce perceives that the line function is weak and unable to manage itself. Rumors about impending reorganizations, layoffs, business strength, and the decline of management capabilities will fly through E-mail, over the FAX machine, and down the assembly line. Line management will no longer be believed if they turn responsibility for their most important business resource over to someone else.

The terminating manager should relate the big picture—corporate sales problems, corporate policy, solutions—to the immediate picture of the people and jobs in his or her department or shop. This may require some practice, role-playing, or maybe even the use of a prepared script. The supervisor may be asked some of the following questions:

- How were people selected to go or stay?
- Were objective techniques such as seniority and classification used?
- Is this a way to get rid of the deadwood?
- When do the layoffs start?
- Will there be a recall?

The most important questions on employees' minds are not always asked directly:

- Am I next?
- Is the company failing?

Until these questions are satisfactorily resolved, either affirmatively or negatively, productivity will decline.

Additional preparation for the terminating manager includes determining the following:

- When the terminations will take place
- Where the terminations will take place
- What paperwork (benefits, final paychecks) will be provided at the termination meeting (usually prepared by HR for the manager)
- Resources available for the departing employees
- Hotline resources available to answer further questions for the firing manager

OTHER FACTORS TO CONSIDER

Need for Confidentiality

The need for confidentiality is a mixed bag. Even in the most open of organizations, certain aspects of the business must be kept confidential. These include the unique details of products under development, negotiations for planned acquisitions, and pending downsizings. A premature, poorly conceived leak of a planned layoff can have a devastating effect on company morale, the corporate reputation in the business community, and future business dealings. One middle manager found out about his company's downsizing and his own planned layoff from one of his customers. He was stunned not only that the customer knew a month in advance but also that his manager denied the truth. As a result, the senior manager missed an opportunity to encourage his direct line manager to support the company through the last days and to provide for a smooth transition for the manager employee and the company. It also was a clear statement to the middle manager and to the grapevine that the customer was more trusted and more important than they were. It bred unnecessary anger and resentment.

Need for Security

There is more fear of violence and sabotage than reality warrants. However, the need for security is important in at least two instances. The first is when an employee targeted for termination is known to have a volatile temper. In this instance, it is appropriate to have a third person, usually the personnel manager, in the room during the termination notification session. It might also be prudent to have the security manager in the next office.

The second instance is when there is danger of sabotage. For example, if there is a possibility that a terminated computer professional might infect the computer system with a virus, the personnel manager might want to assign an associate to escort the employee back to the office and provide assistance in packing up personal belongings and leaving the building.

Table 2 Predictable Reactions to the Emotional Impact of Job Termination

Emotional Reaction	Observable Behavior
Shock	Silence
Immobilization	Blank look, tears
Disbelief	Shocked questioning
Denial	Debate, argument
Anger	Automatic verbal outburst
Bargaining	Pleading
Frustration	Depression
Grieving	Opening up/looking ahead
Resolution	Letting go

Need to Say Goodbye

The need to say goodbye to one's colleagues is compelling, and, except when there is a security risk, every effort should be made to allow the terminated employee to return to the office and say goodbye. If an employee prefers not to return to the workplace when co-workers are there, it might be a good idea to allow the employee to return after hours and provide assistance in cleaning out the office.

Rollercoaster of Emotions

The loss of a job or career is a significant life-disrupting event. Table 2 illustrates the emotional stages that the terminated employee might experience. The manager should become familiar with these normal and predictable reactions to the termination.

GROUP TRAINING SESSION
FOR NOTIFYING MANAGERS

While any manager can read and learn from the previously listed suggestions on how to conduct the termination notification interview, some type of group training is highly desirable. The group training will allow the managers to practice appropriate behaviors as well as to prepare emotionally for a very difficult management task.

Brainstorming. One preliminary group task could involve brainstorming the question, What is the worst thing that can happen in the termination? This will give each manager the opportunity to verbalize and surface hidden fears. A discussion of these fears and the sharing of ideas about appropriate reactions can minimize their chances of disrupting the termination session.

Role-playing. An important feature of the group training is the opportunity to role-play the firing scene with other managers. It can be useful to have an uneasy manager play the role of the notifying manager and a more experienced manager play the role of the employee. The unknown is often more unnerving than the known, and the role-play can allow managers to experience some of the feelings associated with the termination process. Role-playing also allows managers to express their feelings and discomfort. An elementary technique is to ask each manager to write out the feelings they are experiencing on a flip chart. The feelings can then be legitimized by acknowledging and discussing the range of emotions expressed by the group. The managers might then write out the feelings that they think they would experience if they were to be terminated. If necessary, the instructor can probe each manager to express real feelings. When out in the open, these feelings can be acknowledged and dealt with. The group training session will give managers an opportunity to polish their skills in handing over the employee to the individuals who will then work with them: the exit interviewer, the benefits counselor, or the career transition consultant.

Exit interviewer. Most organizations have a practice of conducting an exit interview with every employee who leaves the organization (voluntary terminations, retirements, etc.) The exit interviewer's role involves administrative tasks such as distributing the final check, retrieving company credit cards, and making sure forms are signed and papers are processed. In addition, the exit interviewer, who is usually a personnel or human resources specialist, frequently uses this meeting to gather the employee's views about the organization, its managers, and its personnel practices. In voluntary termination, the exit interview usually is scheduled on the last workday. In layoff situations where termination is effective the same day as the notification, the exit interview may be scheduled for two or three days later to give the employee time to deal with the initial shock of termination.

Benefits advisor.   Large organizations may have professional benefits advisors who conduct a portion of the termination interview activities. While the personnel generalist who conducts the exit interview frequently is seen by terminated employees as representing the company that is firing them, the benefits counselor is often seen as an impartial advisor, almost an ombudsman. The benefits counselor is the one professional in the company who usually has experience in dealing frequently and effectively with people who are experiencing loss. The benefits counselor is the contact person who is called upon to explain insurance benefits to employees or dependents who have just suffered the death of a loved one. They are also very aware that people under emotional stress do not always hear the details about insurance and other benefits. They often take the time necessary to make sure that the employee fully understands the range of benefits available and how to access them. Thus, in some instances, it is the benefits counselor who is the appropriate person for the employee to be handed over to by the notifying manager right after the termination interview. The employee should also receive in writing a detailed listing of the benefits and options available to them at the time of the separation.

The career transition consultant.   This outside resource is particularly useful in instances with long-time, older, or senior employees who are hesitant to express any feeling to the terminating manager. As an outsider, the career transition consultant is seen as a safe person to blow off steam to. The career transition consultant is usually the person who conducts the pretermination training for the notifying manager, exit interviewer, and benefits counselors.

Checklist: Content of the Group Pretermination Training Session for Notifying Managers

❑ Discuss emotions associated with death, divorce, and the job loss model that was presented in table 2.

❑ Discuss and practice methods to be objective and emotionally controlled, while at the same time reflecting genuine and appropriate feelings.

❑ Discuss and practice specific sentences that confirm that the termination is final and irrevocable.

❑ Discuss and role-play reactions and responses to the employee who does not accept the fact that the termination is final and irrevocable.

❑ Discuss how to deal with affected employees who arrive to work in carpools on termination day.

❑ Discuss how to deal with employees who are absent on termination day.

❑ Brief all parties on the items that should be covered with the employee.

- Discuss pay instead of notice, if this is the case.

- Present final check or indicate that it will be given during the exit interview. Explain how vacation pay was calculated.

- Explain severance policy.

- Explain severance pay and how it was calculated.

- Explain COBRA and various insurance options. Have the cost to the employee calculated and be ready to explain sign-up deadlines and procedures. Have a fact sheet available for the employee to take home for family discussion and decision making.

- Discuss commissions due to sales personnel if applicable.

- If appropriate, discuss stock purchase plan, how vesting occurs, and the timetable for exercising options or selling stock.

- Discuss retirement benefits and profit sharing as appropriate.

- Discuss what HR is allowed to say if called for a job reference.

- Discuss referral of employee by manager or benefits counselor to the state employment security office to register for unemployment compensation.

While all of these topics will *not* be included in the dismissal meetings, the manager needs to be prepared to answer them. Employees should also be given written descriptions of the necessary information so that they can begin planning for the future. Often employees do not retain information given to them verbally during a separation meeting.

DEBRIEFING

CEO

It usually falls to the senior organization development specialist, or, in the cases where the organization uses a career transition firm, the senior transition consultant to conduct the debriefing of the CEO.

The debriefing should be conducted as soon as possible after the CEO's meetings with the press, shareholders, managers, and so on. Some useful questions that the person conducting the CEO debriefing can pose are as follows:

- How do you feel your announcement to the press was received?
- How did you feel while you were on camera?
- What have your peers in the business community said about the situation?
- How do you think your corporation is viewed by the business community?
- How did your session with the shareholder go? Did they seem to express confidence or disappointment? What did they express?

- How are the managers who report directly to you taking the news?
- What kind of feedback have you been getting from rank-and-file employees?
- Do you have a feeling for the morale of the organization right now?
- Do you have any idea on how the families are taking it?

These questions should stimulate the CEO to express both opinions and feelings. Many CEOs see their role as just being responsible for the corporate family and neglect their own feelings. These debriefing questions can serve as an opportunity to ventilate their own feelings. In addition to these questions, the debriefer can offer to provide the CEO with a pipeline to what is occurring at the lower levels of the organization. For instance, the debriefer might want to make some of the following statements:

- I will keep you posted on the results of debriefing the managers.
- Let me tell you how a couple of the terminations went.
- I spoke with the exit interviewers and these were the most commonly asked questions.
- The biggest concerns of the continuing employees seem to be…
- If they had to do it again, the managers would like to change…

The debriefer should volunteer to get back to the CEO on a regular and frequent basis as the company proceeds through the downsizing process. It is our experience that the CEO is very interested in this feedback and will even instruct the secretary to "put the debriefer through immediately. Interrupt me if you need to. Squeeze him in if he needs to see me in person."

Senior Managers

As with the CEO, debriefings for senior managers should be held as soon as possible after they have informed the subordinate managers of the downsizing. Questions and statements that can move the debriefing along include the following:

- How did your session go?
- Did they understand the big picture and why the downsizing is necessary?
- Did any issues come up that were difficult to respond to?
- How did you deal with them?

- How did the morale seem to be?
- I think the next thing we need to do is conduct the survivor training in your department. Let's schedule that session for tomorrow.

Firing Managers

The firing managers are the soldiers on the front lines in this matter. They are the ones who confront more expressed anger and experience their own range of feelings more acutely. As with the CEO and senior managers, these debriefings should be held as soon as possible after the manager has informed the employees of the termination. These debriefings should be held with groups of managers, rather than as one-on-one consultations. Some questions and statements that can move the debriefing along are as follows:

- How did your session go?
- How did you feel during your session?
- How do you feel now?
- Anything "unexpected" occur?
- Anything that you expected that didn't come up?
- Will you be seeing the "severed" employee around town?
- How will you act when you see him or her?
- What can you do to help him or her? What are you "willing" to do to help?

In the old days of supervisory training and management development programs, managers were taught interviewing and hiring skills. In this new age of frequent downsizings, it is just as important to learn how to lay off staff humanely and compassionately and to learn how to handle the emotions that firing managers feel. As one manufacturing supervisor said, "I've been with this company for five years and I've never hired anyone. But I have learned how to fire people. No matter how often I do it, I still feel the pain each time."

"Notifiers"

While the bulk of the training for termination is conducted immediately prior to firing day, the training will not be complete without an opportunity for managers to participate in a debriefing of their activities. In this chapter we have stressed the significantly high levels of emotions that are generated during the termination process. Much of the training that we have discussed is focused on assisting with the ventilation and management of the emotions of the employees being terminated. Debriefings are necessary to legitimize the feelings that the managers have experienced in carrying out their tasks as the messengers bearing the bad news. The debriefings can also serve as vehicles for the notifiers to ventilate and dissipate their feelings in a safe and appropriate setting. Finally, the debriefings can serve to provide closure on one aspect of the downsizing, allowing the players to focus on the future and pull together in order to get there.

CONCLUSION

The steps of downsizing require leadership and management. All managers need to be prepared to communicate internally and externally. They are looked to as sources of factual information. The board of directors, the managers, the employees, the media, and the families draw conclusions and construct action steps based on management's communication with them. Not only do they need to be well briefed on what to say and how to say it, but also they need to be debriefed so that they, too, can get on with the next phase of their jobs.

6

The Termination

It was late morning on a crisp and windy day, and Ron Davis could see the pedestrians' steamy breath in the cold air as he drove into the parking lot of Streeter-Haaz Corporation's headquarters building. Ron's boss, Georgia Phillips, division leader of the SK line, had called him yesterday and asked him to come to her office for a planning meeting— something about restructuring in the department. The last time Ron had been at headquarters was several months ago, when he had attended a management training course put on by the training department. The course was called "Disciplining Problem Employees." He had liked that course. He had always avoided disciplining employees for as long as possible. It was a hated task. The instructor had given the managers some clear and simple guidelines to follow: Focus on the job require- ments and the employee's behavior; don't get caught up in the emo- tions; explain what behavior will be required of the employee; ask if the employee understands what is required; make sure that you give the person adequate time to bring performance up to an acceptable level. As Ron entered the elevator, he wondered if the restructuring meant that he could lose some of his people. It would be difficult to operate his shop with less staff. But that didn't worry him as much as having to tell a couple of his employees that their jobs had been eliminated. They didn't have a course for that in management development. As he exited the elevator on the fourth floor, he noticed that the three meeting rooms right before Georgia's office all had Wild West names—the Buffalo Bill Cody room, the Wild Bill Hickok room, and the George Armstrong Custer room. As he waited in Georgia's outer office for her to finish a phone call, he couldn't help but speculate about the reason for the meeting. The restructuring probably meant that he would have to lay off one or two members of his staff, he thought. Well, that's just one of the responsibilities that you take on when you become a manager. Ron was now in Georgia's office sipping on the coffee that her assistant had set down for him before pulling the door shut and disappearing.

Georgia began talking. "Ron, we have a pretty serious business situation that is going to affect our department and you personally. As you know, orders for the SK line are now down over 35 percent, and we can't see the light at the end of the tunnel. I have had to consolidate the three operations groups. The bottom line is that we have had to eliminate your job. I know that this is a shock to..."

THE TERMINATION: TIME, PLACE, AND MANNER

Early in the Week, Late in the Morning

There is a popular phrase in the outplacement business, paraphrased from a popular song and movie from years ago, "Never on Friday." Many managers would prefer to conduct the terminations late Friday afternoon. The manager can then just go home and not have to face the employee or colleagues. When employees are given the bad news at the end of the workweek, they have few opportunities to talk about their emotional reactions to the termination. The results can range from a miserable weekend holed up alone at home, to the abuse of alcohol, and finally to a major depression that can result in suicide. Many career transition consultants recommend that terminations be conducted early in the week, possibly just before noon. This gives the employees the option to leave if they desire or to say goodbye to colleagues.

How Will the Termination Be Conducted?

Terminations should be conducted in a businesslike manner. Usually there should only be two people in the room (the immediate supervisor and the employee). In some instances, especially where there may be complicated compensation or stock option issues, it is appropriate to have one other person called into the room after the manager and the employee have had time to discuss the termination. The person who is called into the room is usually the human resources manager or the employee's next higher level manager.

Where Should the Termination Be Conducted?

A neutral office or meeting room is often the best place to conduct the termination session. If the manager conducts the session in his or her office, it may be difficult to end the session and get on with other business if the employee is in a very emotional state. If the session is conducted in the employee's office, he or she may become embroiled in "turf issues" and order the manager from the office. Other advantages of meeting in a neutral office include the ease of handing over the employee to a career transition counselor (the manager brings the counselor from the next room and then leaves) and the availability of security and controlled access. This is especially critical in a manufacturing facility where meeting rooms often are also storage rooms for spare parts. This is a very sensitive, emotional, and vulnerable time for the employee, and every effort to ensure privacy should be taken.

What About Terminating Large Groups at One Time?

While some companies prefer to call all of the affected employees into the auditorium and give them the bad news, every effort should be made to give the initial notification in private. Most managers have only five to eight direct reports, and only a few of these would be affected by the downsizing. Even in a department that is being heavily affected, each manager can schedule appointments every fifteen to twenty minutes, hand over the employee to a career transition counselor or to the internal benefits or human resources counselor, and move on to the next employee.

Career transition firm managers have a wealth of stories of group termination meetings that were poorly handled or had unnecessarily negative reactions. Several years ago a computer company decided to lay off all employees in one department. They called a meeting of all employees in the auditorium, notified them of their termination, and brought in guards to collect their keys to the facility and company credit cards. Employees were not allowed back in their offices, and boxes of their personal possessions were delivered to them in the parking lot. Is there any mystery why some employees organized a boisterous anticorporate demonstration outside the plant the next day that made the six o'clock news?

Another poorly handled termination occurred at a manufacturing firm's distribution facility. Early in the afternoon, a voice called out over the company's public address system, "Dave Martinez, please come to the human resources office immediately." Dave walked into the human resources office and was handed his termination notice effective that day. He slowly walked back to the facility to tell his friends and colleagues what happened. "Emily Jantz, please come to the human resources office immediately." By the time the third name was called, all work had stopped in the facility as each person waited fearfully for his or her name to be called. Not only was the public announcement of the individual layoff cruel, it also served to alienate the remaining workforce who knew that their names could be called at any moment.

COORDINATING TIMING SCHEDULES FOR TERMINATIONS

If the company finally decides that it must lay off employees, it is critical that communication with employees, managers, and the press be carefully timed. Figure 6 presents a sample timing schedule for conducting terminations.

In addition to communications directed toward the outside world, written communication to affected employees is also important. When communicating to employees, attention should be directed to both content and style of the communication. The style will vary, depending on the culture of the organization.

Schedule

Monday Afternoon

4:30 P.M.

Confidential meeting with all senior managers. CEO tells of decision and steps to be taken for implementation. Importance of confidentiality for security and morale stressed.

5:00 P.M.

Briefing of immediate supervisors of affected employees. CEO makes personal appearance, if possible. Includes a one-hour training session by the career transition consultant on how to give the bad news. Confidentiality for security and morale is stressed.

Tuesday Morning

9:00 A.M.

Immediate supervisors notify each affected employee in private of decision to lay off.

9:30 A.M.

Department managers gather all surviving employees together and notify them of the extent of the layoff and what is being done for those employees who were let go. A survivor briefing is scheduled for the next day. If possible, the CEO makes an appearance.

9:30 A.M.

A news release detailing the particulars of the downsizing is simultaneously hand delivered to all local news media (daily newspaper, business journal, radio station, television station, etc.)

Tuesday Evening

6:00 P.M.

The CEO is interviewed on the six o'clock news.

11:00 P.M.

The human resources manager is interviewed on the 11 o'clock news. The focus is on what is being done to assist the rank-and-file employees in terms of severance and reemployment assistance.

Figure 6   Sample Timing Schedule for Termination Notices

THE TERMINATION SESSION

Many managers are uneasy with terminations and are very slow in getting to the point. This is understandable since they have received absolutely no training on how to conduct the termination process. A checklist for termination and some tips on how to conduct a termination session are presented on the following pages.

Termination Checklist

❏ Date and time
  • Time of week: early in the workweek
  • Time of day: morning
  • Length of severance session: 10 to 15 minutes

❏ Location
  • Neutral office

❏ Who conducts the termination session?
  • Line manager

❏ The terminating session
  • Start with minimal small talk.
  • Get to the point.
  • Tell the person that he or she is being terminated.
  • State the business reason for the termination.
  • State that the decision is irrevocable (and has been reviewed by the highest levels of management).
  • Control your emotions but show feeling.
  • Have written materials available.
  • Hand employee his or her final paycheck (or state where to pick it up).
  • Have reference policy and practices available in writing to be given to the employee.
  • State what the manager will do to personally help.
  • State next steps (e.g., exit interview, meet with career transition firm, attend company job service workshops).

❏ The exit interview
  • Identify who will conduct exit interview.
  • Have the final papers ready for signing.

❏ Written materials to be handed to the exiting employee
  • Notification of last day of work (and/or time of termination)
  • List of benefits available
  • COBRA information
  • Notification of severance pay amount
  • Notification of pay in lieu of notice
  • List of company services available to employee (e.g., job services, counseling services)
  • List of company services available to family (e.g., counseling services)
  • List of community resources available (e.g., job counseling, employment security offices)

Minimize small talk.   Get directly to the point. This is a serious time for both parties. The manager should try to get to the point, often within the first thirty seconds. There may be some difficulty in finding the middle ground between small talk and abruptly saying, "You're terminated." However, it is important to get to the point. In one situation, a personnel manager sat in with a plant manager who was meeting with a long-time employee to tell him he was being laid off. The plant manager and employee had known each other for twenty years. The plant manager chatted about all of their old friends and acquaintances and where they were now. This small talk went on for several minutes and then shifted into the company's need to reduce staff and how tough a decision it was to choose who would be let go. The plant manager then said, "It has sure been nice working with you, and I will miss our opportunities to talk about old times. I will leave you now to talk with the human resources manager." When the plant manager left, the employee turned to the HR manager and said, "I didn't realize that he was leaving. Where is he moving to?" The small talk had deteriorated into not conveying the message. This leads to the next point.

Be clear.   In the above illustration, the manager failed to convey a clear message. The manager should clearly state the facts, "The sales downturn of the past six months has mandated that we reduce our staff. We have considered all other options and have decided to abolish your position. The bottom line is that we will be laying you off effective this Friday."

Stress that the decision is final and irrevocable.   A manager must first be clear in his or her own mind that the decision is final and irrevocable. Then it is important to state this clearly to the employee. This is particularly true of the long-time employee or of the employee who has closely identified with the company. This employee will often be in the denial stage described earlier and will tend to hear what he or she wants to hear. Some long-term and senior employees will want to go up the chain of command and bargain back the job. The best thing that the manager can do for that employee is repeat, gently but firmly, that the decision is indeed final and irrevocable and has been reviewed by senior management. This will save the employee a lot of embarrassment and wasted effort.

Be objective and not blaming.   Use phrases like "the entire job class was eliminated" or "there was a 10 percent across-the-board reduction and your job was among the 10 percent that we lost." Strive to be objective, factual, and quantitative. Do not compare the employee with any other employee who is not being terminated. To do so can lead to an argument about which employee is more deserving to stay and eventually can lead to litigation for unfair layoff practices.

Acknowledge the employee's exhibited feelings.   A termination is one of the most emotion-packed events that any manager or employee will ever experience. Neither party can discount the importance of those emotions. The manager should acknowledge the feelings that are observed in the employee. For instance, the manager might say, "I can see that this has come as a big shock. It's very normal to experience this shock. If you would like to, we can just sit here for a few minutes to deal with it."

Control your emotions but show appropriate feelings.   Keep calm and objective and control your emotions. Let the employee talk and ventilate emotions. Anger is an appropriate feeling that the employee may express. Don't get hooked into the employee's anger, but acknowledge it. Don't ignore it or ask the employee to keep it bottled up inside. This may be a difficult task for the manager to tackle without training. Some role-playing exercises can be very useful in getting the manager comfortable (or at least familiar) with the task of acknowledging strong feelings while keeping his or her own feelings under control.

Have written materials available.   There is a high probability that the employee will not remember very many of the details that are given in the termination session. It is advised that the basics of the termination and the subsequent severance package and benefits be outlined in writing. The manager may even want to read this information out loud to the employee and remind him or her to take it along at the conclusion of the session.

Be clear about the last day to be worked.   Even though it is spelled out in the written material, it may be useful to tell the employee, "You will be paid through the end of the week (or the end of the month, etc.), but you are free to leave right away or at the end of the day."

Be clear about salary continuation and/or severance pay.   Again, even though it is written out, it is best to state the particulars of severance pay. The manager should explain whether the severance is in lieu of notice and whether it will affect immediate eligibility of unemployment compensation benefits. It is also good practice to encourage the employee to visit the state employment security office as soon as possible and apply for benefits, regardless of whether you think the employee qualifies.

Describe what your reference policy will be.   Most companies have a policy that the references for former employees may only be given by the human resources department. The reality of the workplace is that many potential employers will telephone the last supervisor for a verbal reference. Managers should acknowledge this by briefly commenting on what they are willing to tell potential employers. If appropriate, they may want to offer to write a letter of reference.

Person-to-person help.   Many managers and employees have had personally friendly relationships in addition to their official manager–subordinate relationship. This doesn't have to change. Managers can describe what they are willing and able to do personally to help the employee in his or her job search efforts. The manager often has contacts with peers in other companies. An offer to call someone on the employee's behalf or to route a résumé to a colleague is not only easy to do and appreciated but also will help the former employee find a new job faster. Managers need to be clear about not offering to do anything that they are not willing to follow through with and complete.

The exit interview.   The exit interview, generally conducted by a personnel or human resource generalist, is designed to ensure that all the legal and administrative details of the termination are accomplished promptly and accurately. Exit interviews are sometimes done the same day as the termination. This is usually the case when the company wants the employee officially off the payroll as soon as possible. It then serves as the occasion for the employee to be presented with the final paycheck, including vacation pay and severance pay in lieu of notice. If the employee is kept on the payroll, the exit interview may be conducted later that week in order to give the employee time to understand the benefits package and develop specific questions about how to access benefits. In some instances, it is the benefits counselor who is the appropriate person to conduct the exit interview.

The need for security.   The act of termination is loaded with emotion. It puts tremendous emotional stress on the typical manager who must conduct the termination but has never been prepared for this most sensitive of managerial tasks. It is often a devastating emotional blow for the typical employee being laid off. Termination ranks alongside divorce and even the death of a loved one in its emotional shock. While in reality very few terminated employees blow up and put the manager or other employees in danger, it is prudent to be prepared. If the manager is concerned, it might be useful to have a second manager in the termination session. A second option is to have someone from security in the next office, just in case. If the termination is being conducted in an office with a glass panel, the employee should be seated with his or her back to the door, with the security officer positioned to observe any angry physical outburst. If there is a real fear of sabotage (e.g., a production worker could drop a wrench in the machinery or a computer programmer might plant a virus in the computer), the manager might want to assign an assistant to go with the employee to help carry personal belongings out of the facility. In many organizations, there is a growing practice of allowing the employee to return to the office, unaccompanied, to say good-bye to co-workers and leave at noon or the end of the day. In other cases, the affected employee chooses not to return until evening to pick up personal items in private.

Figures 7 and 8 show examples of notification letters that can be handed to employees during the termination session, and a checklist of items that need to be communicated to laid off employees follows.

CONCLUSION

Just as with the hiring process, firing or terminating someone takes planning and practice. The human resources department needs to have all of the supporting documents prepared, schedules need to be set up, and the hiring manager needs to plan where and when the release will take place. It is a difficult time for everyone, yet it needs to be handled with respect for the managers who are on the firing line and the individuals who are getting their notice. The dismissal needs to be handled in the same spirit as that promoted by the organization's mission statement and corporate culture.

STREETER-HAAZ CORPORATION

May 19, 1994

Rosa Romero
2334 Adams Circle
Chadwick, MA 01677

Dear Rosa,

The decline in orders for our SK and MK series products has necessitated a number of cost-cutting measures during the past month. Unfortunately, these measures have not been sufficient to reverse our losses. As a last resort, we have found it necessary to eliminate 176 positions. Your position as Marketing Specialist has been eliminated. While your official date of termination is May 30, 1994, your last day of work is today, May 19, 1994.

Rosa, in recognition of your service, you will receive severance pay based on the following formula: two weeks pay for each full year of service, with a minimum of 4 weeks pay and a maximum of 39 weeks pay. The pay currently due you is calculated as follows:

Pay due on May 30, 1994	$ 2,000.00
Unused vacation due (5.2 days)	$ 1,040.00
Severance pay (7 years = 14 weeks)	$ 14,000.00
Total pay due	$ 17,040.00

Your personal and dependent medical coverage will continue until June 30, 1994, and all other insurance terminates on May 30, 1994. If you would like to continue your medical insurance beyond June 30,1994, you may do so for up to 18 months by paying Streeter-Haaz the monthly premium. After 18 months you must convert to your own individual plan. Attached is an explanation of the COBRA law and a continuation of coverage application form. Complete and submit the form to the personnel

Figure 7   Employee Notification Letter: Long Form

department no later than May 30, 1994, with a check for the amount indicated on the form. Current medical insurance premium rates are as follows:

Employee only	$127.44
Employee and spouse	$285.23
Employee and child	$289.40
Employee, spouse, and children	$447.37

The 1,500-share stock option that you were awarded in 1990 is now 25 percent vested. You have until August 30, 1994, to exercise your option to purchase 375 shares at $.80 per share. If you fail to exercise your option by August 30, 1994, the option will cancel. Our records indicate that you do not participate in the company-sponsored 401(k) retirement program. If this is not the case, contact Elinor Hubbard in the Human Resources Benefits Office.

Streeter-Haaz Corporation would like to assist you in your search for your next position. We have retained Morse Career Transition Services to provide this assistance. Ray Morse and Marianne Clark, both experts in job search, will be conducting a three-day job search workshop beginning next Tuesday, May 22, at the Airport Hilton. In addition, they will provide individual job search coaching as needed for up to 10 weeks. Please call Ray or Marianne at (601) 555-1234 to confirm your workshop attendance. While we hope that you secure employment quickly, we also suggest that you visit the state employment security office to register for unemployment insurance benefits.

Rosa, we appreciate your contributions to Streeter-Haaz and regret that business circumstances have dictated the elimination of your position. I know that you will be an asset to your next employer, and I will be happy to give you the excellent reference that you deserve.

Sincerely,

Stuart Aubret
President and CEO

Figure 7   Employee Notification Letter: Long Form (continued)

STREETER-HAAZ CORPORATION

May 19, 1994

William Baxter
706 Elliott Street
East Chadwick, MA 01670

Dear Bill,

Business conditions require that we eliminate your position as a Store-keeper II effective today, May 19, 1994. You will receive two-weeks pay in lieu of notice. In addition, you will receive four weeks of severance pay. Your final check is attached.

The pay currently due you is calculated as follows:

Pay due on May 19, 1994	$ 100.00
Unused vacation due (5.2 days)	$ 520.00
Pay in lieu of notice (two weeks pay)	$ 1,000.00
Severance pay (two weeks pay)	$ 1,000.00
Total pay due	$ 2,620.00

Your personal and dependent medical coverage will continue until June 30, 1994, and all other insurance terminates on May 30, 1994. You may continue your medical insurance beyond June 30, 1994, by paying Streeter-Haaz the monthly premium. Attached is an explanation of the COBRA law and a continuation of coverage application form. Complete and submit the form to the personnel department no later than May 30, 1995, with a check for the amount indicated on the form. Check with the human resource department for specifics.

Our records indicate that you do not participate in the company-sponsored 401(k) retirement program.

While we hope that you secure employment quickly, we suggest that you visit the state employment security office to register for unemployment insurance benefits.

Figure 8   Employee Notification Letter: Short Form

A job search workshop will be held on Monday, May 21, at the Airport Hilton. Please call (601) 555-1234 to confirm your workshop attendance. Bill, we appreciate your contributions to Streeter-Haaz and regret that business circumstances have dictated the elimination of your position. I know that you will be an asset to your next employer and wish you good luck in your job search.

Sincerely,

Sara Worthington

Sara Worthington
Materials Manager

Figure 8   Employee Notification Letter: Short Form (continued)

Checklist of Items to Be Communicated to Terminated Employees

❑ The business reality

❑ Layoff or job elimination

❑ Last day of work

❑ Date termination is effective

❑ Pay in lieu of notice

❑ Severance pay formula
   • Lump sum
   • Pay continuation

❑ Amount of current pay due

❑ Unused vacation pay accrued

❑ Continuation of benefits
   • Medical insurance
   • Life insurance
   • Dental insurance
   • Vision care
   • Disability insurance

❑ COBRA regulations

❑ How payment is arranged

❑ Necessary forms

- ❏ Stock options
  - • How much vested?
  - • Deadline for exercising option
- ❏ Retirement plan
- ❏ Unemployment insurance
- ❏ Job transition assistance

PROVIDING FOR THE DISPLACED WORKER

7

External Transition Resources

Several weeks before Stuart Aubret had made his companywide announcement regarding the layoffs at Streeter-Haaz, Christina Perugia,
Senior Vice President of Human Resources, had asked Dr. Eugene Smith,
her training and development manager, and Delia Brown, her employment manager, to meet with her in her office. Prior to this, Christina had
met weekly with the task force on staffing. She and the other senior
officers had developed their layoff rationale and had laid out the basic
plan for releasing 176 employees. This includeded first-line supervisors,
clerical and administrative staff, and 132 hourly workers, including
technicians, maintenance staff, and production workers from the SK line.
Some of the production and maintenance staff were union workers. Also
slated for layoff was the SK line's Senior Vice President of Sales and
Marketing.

Now that Christina, Gene, and Delia were moving toward implementation stages, they felt overwhelmed by the enormity of the task. How
could they quickly and humanely move 176 people out of the organization? Who could provide the career search and coaching services for all
of these levels of employees?

As the meeting progressed, they laid out their strategy:

- Christina would contact the local Private Industry Council (PIC).
- Gene would decide what career workshops and job assistance
  services his staff could provide. He would also contact outplacement
  firms, nonprofit agencies, employment agencies, independent career
  counselors, and the local community and four-year college career
  programs.

- Delia would develop a strategy for transferring employees internally.

As they walked down the hall, they glumly acknowledged that the results of their efforts would directly affect the working lives of 176 people, their families and the community, and the future of the company.

Christina knew that the magnitude of Streeter-Haaz's layoffs meant that the company must follow certain federal legislative requirements. Colleagues at other companies had told her that the local PIC would be a good source of information. She wondered about who those people were and what they could do for her. After talking with the local PIC manager, she put together her report.

FEDERAL, STATE, AND LOCAL ASSISTANCE PROGRAMS

Congress has enacted legislation to help dislocated workers move into new jobs and new careers. The legislation includes two laws: the Worker Adjustment and Retraining Notification Act (WARN) and the Economic Dislocation and Worker Adjustment Assistance Act (EDWAAA).

Worker Adjustment and Retraining Notification Act

The Worker Adjustment and Retraining Notification Act, which has been discussed in some detail in chapter 4, was enacted in 1988. It applies to employers with 100 or more full-time workers and requires a sixty-day notice of a mass layoff or plant closing.

The intent of the legislation is to forewarn the company's employees, other local employers, regional businesses, the political community, and the state and federal government that a large number of employees soon will be on the street. Obviously, a large layoff affects a large number of people and businesses: local grocery and retail shops, religious organizations, community service people, and the state unemployment agency. It also affects all of the company's suppliers and customers. When this legislation was being debated, there was considerable fear expressed by employers that if their employees knew sixty days in advance that the plant would be closing, they would resort to such actions as leaving their jobs early, lowering productivity, or even sabotaging the plant. The worst fears have not become reality. What the WARN legislation has done is to force companies to plan strategically how to communicate and work with their employees and their unions before and during the layoff, how to work with their suppliers, and how to work with the community to maintain their public image. Employers generally work with their employees to give them time off to look for other jobs, and, in exchange, the employees come to work when they're supposed to (i.e., they are less likely to call in sick or not show up for work).

The Economic Dislocation and
Worker Adjustment Assistance Act

This act replaces the old Title III of the Job Training Partnership Act (JTPA) and challenges state and local government, business, and labor to form partnerships to collaboratively increase dislocated and unemployed workers' job skills and employability and to help them become reemployed as quickly as possible.

The EDWAAA, administered by the U.S. Department of Labor, conveys its funding support through state, district, and local agencies.

The State Job Training Coordinating Council (SJTCC). This agency shares decision-making authority for many state functions with the governor in an advisory capacity. The council, appointed by the governor, must have a nongovernmental chair and must draw one-third of its membership from business and industry (including business representatives from local Private Industry Councils), at least one-fifth from state legislatures and state agencies, and at least one-fifth from other relevant interests. The state council plans, coordinates, and monitors state employment and training programs and services. It does not operate programs or provide direct services.

Service Delivery Areas (SDAs). These are the districts within a state through which direct job training services are delivered. SDAs may include more than one local government area, but may not split local political jurisdictions. Each SDA has a Private Industry Council. States must pass through 78 percent of their allocations to SDAs.

The Private Industry Council (PIC). This agency shares overall policy and oversight responsibility for local programs with locally elected officials. The PIC represents local business leaders (who must make up a majority of its members), educational institutions, organized labor rehabilitation agencies, community-based organizations, economic development agencies, and local employment services. Whenever possible, half of the business organizations represent small businesses.

PRIVATE INDUSTRY COUNCILS

These councils are accountable to the city and/or county government in which they reside and to the regional employers. They have three masters: (a) the federal and state EDWAAA-funded agencies, (b) the public entities that want to help their constituents find and keep jobs, and (c) the PIC board of employers, union representatives, and local agencies who want to ensure the regional job health of the community. Every PIC also has three customers: (a) the company that is going through a major downsizing or plant closure, (b) the out-of-work client who wants a job, and (c) the employer who wants to hire qualified, trained, ready-to-work employees. As a result, each PIC not only provides a base level of services throughout the country but also develops customized services to meet the unique employment needs of its area. For example, the North Valley Private Industry Council (NOVA PIC) in Sunnyvale, California, serves the defense industry and the Silicon Valley high-tech firms. The NOVA PIC used to train displaced cannery workers to work on the silicon chip assembly lines. Now they are working with defense industry engineers and scientists who are used to working with three- to four-year deadlines and zero level error rates to transfer their technical skills to the commercial world with three- to four-month deadlines and a higher tolerance level of error.

Individual PIC funding is based on the level of unemployment in that district. Those with higher levels of unemployment receive more state pass-through funds.

How It Works

The source of the funding for the direct service programs is the Job Training Partnership Act (JTPA). Services such as training, job development, job search, and job placement are provided to those who are economically disadvantaged or who are displaced workers.

Funding for the program is channeled from the federal government through the states, to the PICs, and then to companies, unions, and service providers. Governors have broad authority over eligibility, program planning and administration, resource distribution, and provision of service. The JTPA is a decentralized system administered at a state level by SJTCCs and at the local level by PICs. There are fifty-seven SJTCCs and over 650 PICs throughout the United States.

Services Provided by PICs

When a company is about to release significant numbers of employees, it needs to work with their local PIC to follow the WARN guidelines. What kinds of services can be expected?

Mike Curran, director of the NOVA PIC in Sunnyvale, California, comments on the kinds of services his office can offer Silicon Valley employers.

> With WARN in effect, we're called first. We go to the company and ask them what they want to provide in the way of employment services for their staff and find out what kinds of services they need from us. Then immediately we do three things: (a) find employers who want to hire *now*, (b) find out if employee skills in the downsizing company are transferable to another industry, and (c) find out if employees need to be retrained to complement their current skills or if they need to learn a new skill. The last option is the most expensive and time-consuming one.

Based on their federal mandate, PICs are expected to be proactive in their efforts to work with downsizing companies. They prefer to work with the management during the early decision-making phases to ease the process for the company and for their employees. Every state is expected to establish regional or local *rapid response teams*, which provide a group of skilled career counselors who are willing and able to immediately set up shop on the company site. PIC administrators work with the company's management to plan and manage the layoff. They work with the local unions and, in very large plant closures, with several agencies and private career counseling or outplacement firms to coordinate services for the full range of displaced employees. PIC counselors and trainers conduct workshops on how to write a résumé, conduct a job search, and prepare for an interview. They can provide assessment programs to determine a worker's skill level (important for job transferability) and can recommend or provide job training programs. While PICs work with all levels of employees, they are primarily known for their efforts with blue collar workers and first-line supervisors.

PICs also provide assessment and job search services for smaller company downsizings and for individuals. They have a large number of programs (with local variations) aimed primarily at the low-skilled displaced worker, the parent receiving help from Aid to Families With Dependent Children, the homeless, the senior citizen who wants to supplement social security benefits, and the disadvantaged. At the other end of the financial and managerial spectrum, some PICs coordinate with state employment security offices to provide a professional job club. ProMatch, led by the Sunnyvale, California, office of the state employment security agency and coordinated with the NOVA PIC, meets every Wednesday morning in the Sunnyvale City Council chambers. There is a five- to six-week waiting list to join and a time limit of six months in the club. During the spring of 1994, there were 260 active members.

Staff members of PICs are degreed career counselors, job developers, workshop leaders, and intake counselors who must be familiar with all the eligibility requirements. Like most businesses, they supplement their core workforce with part-time or contract staff and subcontract vocational training to local profit and nonprofit businesses.

What is the cost to the employer or to the dislocated job seeker who walks in off the street? While there are no direct charges to either employer or employee, this service has been paid for with tax dollars. Roberts P. Jones, assistant secretary of the Department of Labor during the Bush administration, commented in a speech to the International Association of Outplacement Professionals that the 1990–91 funding for these services stood at $400 million. Because these agencies have been successful in meeting the needs of employers, employees, and the community, and their need has been so great due to corporate and public agency downsizings, funding is increasing. The federal budget increased from $421 million in 1991 to $1.5 billion for 1995.

CAREER TRANSITION AND OUTPLACEMENT FIRMS

The professional career transition and outplacement business is an industry comparable in size and financial base to publicly managed

PICs. While they provide some of the same services as PICs, they traditionally focus on the management and executive levels of exiting employees and provide more consulting services to management to assist the survivors after the downsizing. They have provided during the last three years, and will continue to provide throughout the 1990s, an increasing range of services to middle and first-level managers and blue collar workers. Generally, they do not provide retraining for the displaced or for those with low incomes.

Outplacement was first developed as a distinct business in the 1960s when Saul Gruner, an executive recruiter, was asked by Humble Oil to help place a few senior managers outside of the company. By the late 1970s, there were four or five companies in the business of outplacement. With the high number of mergers, acquisitions, and takeovers in the early 1980s and the high number of layoffs and downsizing companies in the late 1980s and early 1990s, the business has blossomed. Kennedy Publications, which publishes the industry directories, notes that in 1993 there were 250 firms whose primary business was outplacement, not including a number of outplacement firms that provide services occasionally. The term *outplacement* is a confusing one. People in this business don't place anyone (i.e., they're not recruiters, headhunters, or placement agencies). The firms that specialize in helping companies and their exiting employees through the transition process now consistently refer to themselves as *career transition firms.*

The clients of career transition firms are companies and organizations, not individuals. The firms work with organizations to help plan the reduction in size of the workforce and with the employees who are being dismissed. In addition, they are now increasingly working with management after the downsizing(s) to provide organizational development services to refocus the organization's strategic mission and to get the remaining workforce reorganized, remotivated, and back working again. The major distinction between career transition firms and career counseling firms is that the paying client for the former is the organization and for the latter is the individual.

There are three basic kinds of career transition firms, which are defined more by size than by service: the big firms, the midsized firms, and the smaller local or specialized firms. The one thing they all have in common is that they provide career assessment and job search services. They do not find jobs for individuals; they teach them how to find a job.

Criteria for Transition Organization Selection

Downsizing companies, when enlisting the services of a career transition firm, are well advised to select a firm that meets the following criteria:

- The ability to work with a diverse group of candidates, both men and women, the disabled, and persons of different racial backgrounds and with diverse occupational specialties
- A diverse workforce
- A track record of candidates who are hired
- The ability to provide termination planning for one individual or a whole group
- Competent, capable, well-trained counselors who have work experience in fields related to the downsizing organization
- The immediate availability of a counselor

Other criteria, based on company needs, include the following:

- Ability to advise companies on the most effective and humane way to manage the downsizing process
- Knowledge of the company field (e.g., engineering, medicine, government)
- Ability to provide survivor training and organizational consulting services after the initial downsizing effort

The Big Three

The "Big Three" in the U.S. career transition business are Drake Beam Morin, Right Associates, and Lee Hecht Harrison. In 1990, Kennedy Publications published *An Analysis of the Outplacement Consulting Business in North America*. This was the first analysis of the career transition business. In 1993, Kennedy Publications cited revenues for the three firms at a combined total of approximately $292 million out of a total of $750 million for the entire U.S. outplacement industry. Drake Beam Morin is the largest with revenues of $140 million; Right Associates is next in size with approximately $110 million in worldwide revenues; and Lee Hecht Harrison follows with $42 million in U.S. revenues. This can be compared with the U.S. Federal Government's

1993 budget of $750 million and the 1995 projected budget of $1.4 billion for expenditures for downsizing assistance.

The Big Three provide a full scope of services to clients: They advise managers from the inception of the layoff idea through the pretermination planning and analysis, assist with public relations efforts, train supervisors and managers who do the actual firing, and provide a wide range of individual and group job search services for executives, middle managers, supervisors, and hourly and blue collar workers. The services can be contracted separately or as a full package. (See chapter 8 for further discussion.)

The Midsized North American Firms

In the taxonomy of midsized firms, there are two variations. The first is a single company that has several branch offices in key locations throughout North America. The second is a consortium of independent local entrepreneurial companies that operate as a nationwide service provider. Two in this category are Outplacement International and the Lincolnshire Group, Inc. The companies within the consortium have a common philosophical base and set common standards of quality. When asked to outplace large numbers of employees or those living in distant places, they will assist each other with the caseload or refer clients to a member company. In 1991, Outplacement International, with twenty member firms and forty offices, was the fourth largest outplacement entity in the United States.

According to the Kennedy report, the next nine largest North American firms are the following:

- Challenger, Gray and Christmas
- Murray Axmith & Associates (Canada and Australia)
- King, Chapman, Broussard & Gallagher
- Peat Marwick Stevenson Kellogg (Canada)
- Jannotta Bray & Associates
- Manchester
- Mainstream Access
- EnterChange
- Fuchs, Cuthrell

Their impact on the industry cannot be measured in sales revenue alone. They include some of the major founders and leaders in the industry, and they heavily influence the direction and future of the career transition business.

The Big Three, the consortia, and some of the midsized firms can relatively easily assemble a team of people to work on large projects, such as a plant closing. They also conduct major studies on layoffs, the length of time to become reemployed, rehire rates by age groups and gender, salary comparisons of former and new positions, employee and business trends, and the kinds of businesses experiencing downsizing and those most likely to increase or decrease in size in the future. The reports are readily available to clients and prospective clients. Right Associates conducts annual survey interviews of human resource managers and business leaders at the Society for Human Resource Management and other similar professional national conventions and then publishes the reports in summary in "The Right Report," as well as in the book *Lessons Learned* (Right Associates, 1992).

Local and Smaller Firms

Some of these companies provide "niche-based" consulting, for example, working with difficult clients or senior executive officers or focusing on specific professional fields such as science, education, or sales and marketing. They provide a range of services based on individual capabilities and can be extraordinarily useful because of their knowledge of local or niche markets. Some have working arrangements with firms in other parts of the country and can provide assistance on a wider basis.

International Firms

Career transition is not just a phenomenon in the United States. There is a considerable amount written about the internationalization of business and the global marketplace. Inevitably, there are also businesses worldwide that are downsizing. Ford announced in the spring of 1991 that they were laying off 30 percent of their workforce in Europe—a number that translates to 6,300 employees. The International Association of Outplacement Professionals (IAOP), a membership association that focuses on professional development of the individual outplacement consultant (in-house, with a firm, or independent), has members in seventeen international regions, including Asia, Central and Latin America, Canada, and Europe. The Association of Outplacement Consulting Firms International (AOCFI), an organization of outplacement firms, includes member firms or branches throughout Great Britain, Europe, Asia, and South America. Now that there has been a thaw in Eastern Europe, career transition firms are considering opening new branches in those regions.

Pauline Hyde is well known in Ireland and England. Murray Axmith & Associates has offices in Canada (its home base) and Australia. The Big Three career transition firms based in the United States (Lee Hecht Harrison, Right Associates, and Drake Beam Morin) have international offices as well. The issues, the laws, the taxation and benefits questions, and the cultural and language differences all contribute to a need for transition services that can specifically serve the needs of clients in their home locations around the world.

The combined total revenues of the private U.S. career transition firms are comparable to that spent by the federal government through the JTPA programs in 1990. The U.S. federal government is now multiplying its budget exponentially to handle the newly unemployed and the long-term unemployed. While these are the largest service providers for organizations, there are additional resources available for employers and candidates. The first of these are the national and local nonprofit groups.

National and Local Nonprofit Groups

The clients of nonprofit groups are usually individuals rather than organizations. They focus their attention on getting people back to work through job search assistance or retraining.

One of their strongest assets are the job clubs. Most people in the job search business assert that the most effective way to find a new job is through networking. And many also assert that an effective means of exponentially increasing networking contacts is through job support groups. They go by many names and have a variety of sponsors. Nonprofit job groups typically are sponsored by local chambers of commerce, the YMCA and YWCA, religious organizations such as the Jewish Vocational Service, career resource centers, and state employment agencies.

Companies that want to maintain a positive relationship in the community and with their current—as well as their former—employees often encourage the development of local job support groups. Many firms will list the names, addresses, and phone numbers of local contacts as part of the list of resources for exiting employees.

Nonprofit groups serve the full range of out-of-work employees. Forty Plus focuses on executives and managers who are over the age of forty; Operation ABLE focuses on the full spectrum of older workers (e.g., disabled and poorly trained as well as those who were in mid- to senior-level management positions). Executives and managers who either are not given the opportunity to use career transition firms or whose transition contract or company severance package has run out may turn to the nonprofit groups. Some managers make the nonprofits or executive PIC-sponsored programs their first choice for the vast array of networking that is immediately available.

FORTY PLUS.   Forty Plus is the longest established and probably the best known of the national nonprofit job search networks and support groups. It was founded in 1939 and has fifteen branches in the United States. Its mission is to assist out-of-work managers and executives who are over the age of forty with finding a job. There are no paid positions in the organization. It is based on the idea of self- and group-help. Networking, long before it became a popular and fashionable idea, was one of its chief virtues. Anyone who wants information about a potential employer simply has to stand up in the general meeting and ask, and someone will have worked there recently or know someone who works there now. Members pay a membership fee and monthly dues and must contribute time on a weekly basis to the group. In exchange, they receive job search assistance, use of phones, a place to swap job information, workshops on résumé writing and interviewing, and information about companies. Contacts and friendships formed in these groups can last for years. Many former job seekers are willing to read résumés and talk to the newly displaced executives. They remember what it was like.

OPERATION ABLE.   Operation ABLE (Ability Based on Long Experience) is a Chicago-based nonprofit agency founded in 1977 whose mission is to provide employment opportunities for older adults. Its slogan is "Fifty-five is the speed limit, not the age limit." Funding comes from a blend of federal and state JTPA sources, corporate contracts, and contributions from corporations, foundations, individuals, and the United Way. Major programs include job and training opportunities for older economically disadvantaged and dislocated workers, corporate services such as temporary agencies for clerical workers, career counseling and assessment programs, and the Upward Mobility Program conducted for the American Federation of State, County, and Municipal Employees (AFSCME) and the State of Illinois. An example of the kind of program that Operation ABLE can put together is the consortium approach they used to help AT&T's unionized workers develop their careers. The 1990–91 Operation ABLE Annual Report describes the consolidated approach that was used:

> The Alliance for Employee Growth and Development, a cooperative venture of AT&T, the Communication Workers of America (CWA), and the International Brotherhood of Electrical Workers (IBEW), selected Operation ABLE in 1989 to administer and implement its employee development programs through two Employee Resource Centers.... At no cost to the employee we worked these past two years with 13 Alliance Local Committees around the state to provide more than 1,400 union represented AT&T employees with a chance to grow and develop their careers.

> ABLE's program for the Alliance serves as a model for the country, and is part of a national effort by AT&T and the CWA and IBEW to help AT&T employees get the training and support they need to keep them employed in or out of AT&T.

> Service provided Alliance members during fiscal years 1990/91 included career testing and assessment, career counseling, "Return to Learn" programs, financial transition seminars, entrepreneurial programs, and job search training and placement assistance.

There are now five Operation ABLE offices in the Chicago area and seven affiliated agencies in the national ABLE network: Arkansas ABLE, Careers Encore–Los Angeles, Operation ABLE of Greater Boston, Operation ABLE of Michigan–Southfield, Operation ABLE of Southeast Nebraska–Lincoln, Senior Employment Services–New York City, and the Vermont Associate.

For-profit Groups

Another career transition service available to individuals is through the for-profit organizations. Individuals pay for a range of services from résumé-writing assistance to individualized counseling services to group meetings.

THE FIVE O'CLOCK CLUB.   This club was first formed in 1978 to meet the needs of New York managers and executives who were in a job search and who did not have access to company-sponsored career transition firm services. With the success of the New York Club, founder Kate Wendleton wrote a well-received book, *Through the Brick Wall,* and is now franchising Five O'Clock Clubs throughout the United States. The premise is that managers and professionals meeting together to provide networking, emotional support, and job search and company information will move more quickly into their next successful position. Unlike self-help groups, leadership of the weekly meetings is provided by professional career counselors. Participants pay a relatively low amount for a defined series of group meetings. Additional one-on-one services are also available. No job guarantees are made; however, their success rate is fairly strong.

There are numerous other local and national organizations that provide services to individuals. Most offer individualized résumé assistance, job search techniques, and coaching services. There is a wide range of fees charged for the services.

Executive Recruiters, Employment Agencies, and Temporary Employment Agencies

It may appear peculiar to look at executive recruiters and employment agencies as a source of job search services. However, since their focus is on the corporate client who is seeking specific types of employees, they often know the jobs that are available and the skills and abilities that are required by the hiring companies. These company services are usually paid by the hiring company, not the candidate. The employer will use their services to find their next permanent or temporary employees.

In some management, executive, and professional circles, executive recruiters, known more familiarly as *headhunters,* are seen as saviors. After the first shock of being fired, the next thought that passes through many senior staff members' minds is, I'll bet a headhunter will get me a new job—and an even better one than I had before! While it's true that executive recruiters know about a lot of job openings (good and otherwise), they make their money by serving the needs of the employer, not the job hunter. John Lucht, in his book *Rites of Passage at $100,000+* , writes one of the best guides to understanding the role of the contingency and the retained recruiter and how job hunters can work most effectively with them. Farsighted individuals and those who have been terminated before start developing their relationships with recruiters years in advance in preparation for the next layoff. But then, these well-prepared and proactive employees are the ones who will have the least difficulty getting a new position. Sometimes downsizing companies will make contact with recruiters for certain selected individuals just to help out their conscience and to help individuals move on. One of the harder hit industries in the early 1990 recession is the executive recruiter field—some of them are out looking for work, too.

What executive recruiters are to the professional and managerial world, employment agencies are to the hourly workforce. Like recruiting firms, employment agencies usually have their fees paid by companies. Some will also work with walk-ins and charge them a fee for job placement. Most employment agencies market particular skills: accounting, sales, word processing, or data entry, for example. They are looking for people who are already skilled or who have skill levels that can be easily increased through onsite company training.

New temporary employment agencies are popping up as a growth industry. There are even a few that advertise that they will provide temporary executives—presidents, chief financial officers, or chief operating officers—on a short-term basis.

Kelly Services has provided temporary workers in the areas of office, marketing, technical, and light industrial work for many years. In 1990, they had 580,000 employees working out of 950 company-owned offices worldwide. Their copyrighted Kelly PC-Pro training system provides free training to more than 6,000 temporary employees weekly in word processing and spreadsheet packages. As one of the largest employers in the world, they have to pay attention to employer demands for particular job skills, and they are willing to train their workforce to meet the need.

Manpower, Inc. is another large temporary agency that employs 1.5 million people annually through its 1,600 offices in 34 countries. In a study they conducted in 1990, 15 percent of the 15,000 companies surveyed noted that they will be hiring more employees; another 16 percent expect to lay off employees. And while contract/temporary employees are often the first to be let go, they are increasingly being used by larger companies to buffet the ebb and flow of production demands. For downsizing employers, temporary agencies can be a resource to pick up some of their exiting staff, to train or retrain them, and to employ them into other companies.

In the career counseling, career transition, and job search business, there is much emphasis on the differences between the services these individuals provide and their professional capabilities. The range of titles is enormous: career counselor, career consultant, career coach, career planner, transition manager, outplacement consultant, job consultant, job developer, executive career coach, career guidance counselor, retirement or preretirement planner, reinventor, and others.

It is more important to know the skills and capabilities of career consultants than to focus on their titles. See table 3 for a comparison of skills of professionals who provide career assistance to outplaced employees. As an aside, these same titles are used by the federal government, nonprofit agencies, corporations, and private job search firms with the same level of confusion.

For many people, there is a distinction between career counselors and job search/outplacement specialists.

Career counselors generally focus on assisting individuals or groups with identifying their values and abilities, their interests, and their career direction. Companies that believe in developing their employees, want to rekindle restless staff, and/or want to help employees and managers find a good long-term job fit based on mutual needs and talents will hire career counselors to assist in the process. Most career counselors stop at this stage. Some will provide résumé writing and job search assistance. A smaller number will work with individuals throughout the search process until the person makes a transition into another job.

The general career counselor sees a wide range of clients with a wide range of needs. The individual client might be a high school or college graduate looking for a first time job, someone looking to explore options, a retiree wanting employment that will not violate Social Security requirements, or individuals who have been terminated from their job. By contrast, the career transition counselor focuses on the narrow niche of out-of-work candidates who are actively seeking employment (a few are looking toward retirement or academic reentry). The psychological and financial needs of the unemployed are generally more demanding than the needs of the general career counselee. While there is a common base of skills and knowledge required, career transition counselors must be able to handle emotional venting, depression, and the sense of urgency most laid-off workers feel.

Table 3 A Comparison of the Skills of Professionals Who Provide Career Assistance to Outplaced Employees

Skill Area	Career Counselor	Outplacement Consultant	Job Search Coach
Advising on planning a downsizing	No	Yes	No
Training the terminators	No	Yes	No
The training survivor	No	Yes	No
Ventilation of feelings	Yes	Yes	No
Administering assessment instruments	Yes	Yes	Maybe
Interpreting assessment instruments	Yes	Yes	Maybe
Exploration of options	Yes	Yes	Yes
Development of a career focus	Yes	Yes	Yes
Résumé preparation	Maybe	Yes	Yes
Career strategy development	Maybe	Yes	Yes
Contact network development	Maybe	Yes	Yes
Targeting employers	Maybe	Yes	Yes
Using employment agencies	Maybe	Yes	Yes
Using the telephone	No	Yes	Yes
Writing cover letters	No	Yes	Yes
Teaching interview skills	No	Yes	Yes
Evaluating job offers	No	Yes	Yes
Salary negotiation	No	Yes	Yes

Most importantly, the job search counselor and career transition consultant are hired by a company to provide job search services. The expected outcome is a new job. The career counselor may be hired by either the company or by the individual ("retail career counseling"). While both the job search counselor and the more general career counselor focus on the three phases of personal career development (self-assessment, exploration of options, and job search techniques), the emphasis for career transition consultants is on the job search strategy, setting up informational interviews, and networking for contacts and job interviews. In brief, they are doing everything possible to help the candidate land a new job.

The range of services and counselor capabilities is enormous. All of them can be useful to a corporation, depending on what is needed. The first step is to figure out the employee's needs, and the second is to check the credentials, services, and reputation of prospective career counselors.

Career Consulting Firms and Other Available Services

Novations, Inc., based in Orem, Utah, is a career consulting business that has worked with many companies over the past number of years. They have produced several research studies, particularly on the careers of scientists and engineers. There are several other equally well-known firms (Career Research and Testing of San Jose, California, The Career Development Team of Greenwich, Connecticut, and Beverly Kaye and Associates of Sherman Oaks, California) that can design career development programs that are particularly effective for companies desiring to improve the skills and career health of their employees over a two-year period or longer. Most are not in the business of downsizing; however, their knowledge of career development has shaped the assessment and job search activities of outplacement consultants.

Unions

Labor unions are traditionally seen as management antagonists crying, "Jobs at any cost!" and "We want more!"—more job security, higher wages, less regular shift time (and more overtime), and higher benefits. Faced with the reality of downsizing and layoffs, union groups are working with management and the community to ease the transition from worker to candidate to reemployed. It is a federal requirement that a union representative be on every PIC board.

College Programs

Four-year colleges and universities, two-year community colleges, and business and trade schools have provided career counseling services for their students for many years. Many also offer services to their alumni or to the community at large. Services generally include classes as well as individual consultation in values and interest inventories, skills and abilities assessment, résumé writing, interviewing skill development, and job search techniques. For many years, the academic world has set up recruitment schedules that allow for companies and students to meet each other. Most keep close track of how many of their students have been hired, in what fields, and in which companies.

College career classes and services are now part of the business of the academic world and are generally available, on a contract basis, to companies for their employees. AT&T in Pleasanton, California, contracted with the local Las Positas Community College to provide a multiweek career course for their telephone operators and general clerical staff. The groups of twenty met on Saturdays for an eighteen-hour course that included one hour of individual career consulting with the state accredited community college instructor.

Four-year college and two-year community college career staff include counselors, workshop leaders, and library technicians. One of the strengths of the college programs is their well-stocked libraries of career resources. Another is their low cost. Generally they are better known for their assessment and general guidance programs rather than for the follow-through challenge of the actual job search. Also, since they are in the education business, they often see the solution to job dislocation as reeducation—that is, signing up for classes at that institution. With the enormous influx of students into the community colleges, many of these institutions now limit the on-campus career centers to enrolled students. Some two-year colleges still open their career center doors to the community-at-large.

CONCLUSION

Companies have a wide range of resources available to them, their displaced workers, and their current strategic workforce. Companies can develop consortia and partnerships among the various resources. For example, they can request that private outplacement firms work with all levels of managers and professionals, that PICs work with blue collar staff, and that corporate career consultants develop in-house career development programs for their strategic staff.

8

Designing a Program for Outplaced Employees

Steve Moir, Senior Vice President of Sales and Marketing, was early for his meeting with his boss, Stuart Aubret. He adjusted his tie, brushed the vest on his pin-striped suit, and smoothed back his hair as he strolled across the lobby of the corporate headquarters. The fountain in the center of the courtyard bubbled over the dozen or so good-luck coins that had been tossed into the pool. When he got out of the elevator, he was lost in thought, reviewing his proposal for a new marketing plan for their largest European customer. He and his staff had been working on it for months, and now it was ready to go. Stuart was waiting for him.

"Steve, as you know, business has been rocky for the past three quarters. As part of the change in corporate direction, you will be laid off as of Friday this week. I've prepared a packet of information for you concerning your severance pay and benefits. I've also arranged for Ray Morse of the Morse Outplacement Firm to work with you. He's in the next room waiting to meet you."

That was it. No more job. No more worrying about the marketing plan. Steve was numb. He wasn't sure that he really understood what had been said to him. He was no longer an employee; his head was spinning; he was now an "outplacement candidate."

Waiting for him in the next room was an outplacement consultant. What kind of help could he expect? What was this outplacement all about?

EASING THE TRANSITION
FOR TERMINATED WORKERS

Everyone is interested in helping the terminated worker quickly find new employment: the company, the community, the job transition services, and the out-of-work employees and their families. Companies that facilitate the process at every level will retain their good name in the business and civic community by helping their employees move more quickly and easily into their next positions.

Table 4 gives the reader a sparse outline of the emotional roller coaster that a candidate experiences in a six-month job search. The following description of a candidate's job transition is intended to give a more personal glimpse of the process from the human perspective.

Jerry: A True Tale

Jerry had been with Unisys for twenty-two years. He was part of the company when it was called Burroughs and survived the initial merger with Sperry Univac. Just two years later he was offered a new job as a middle manager for customer relations—the kind of job he really liked—working with customers and problem solving with them and his staff. In the fall, there were rumblings that Unisys was in financial trouble. Then it was announced: layoffs for 10,000 people nationwide. Jerry knew that he was part of the old gang that had been absorbed and he knew that there weren't very many of them left. As the newest in the office, he also had less tenure than some others. He survived the first pass. Some of his colleagues and friends didn't. Now there was more work than ever to do and fewer people to do it. It meant longer hours and waiting for the other shoe to drop. How was he feeling? He had been with Unisys for a long time and he really liked the idea of retiring from the company with a good pension. He was also restless. He had been doing this job for some time and he was a little bored, but not enough to make a change.

The rumors kept flying. The regional manager was due to arrive in mid-January for an inspection. And the district manager, Jerry's boss, was getting more and more agitated. By early January, Jerry had a bet going with one of the other managers, Anne. Anne had a dentist appointment on the morning that the regional manager was scheduled to arrive. If their boss allowed her to keep the appointment, then Anne knew she wouldn't be fired. And Jerry knew he would be. Anne was given the OK to take off. Jerry didn't tell his wife about the bet. That morning, at 3:00 A.M., Jerry got a call from one of his

Table 4 Typical Job Search Cycle

Week	Activity	Emotional Stage
1	Termination, ventilation	Shock, disbelief, immobilization, anger
2	Writing accomplishments	Elation, denial, hope, optimism
3	Assessment, résumé	Frustration, hope
4	Contacts list development	Frustration
5	Phone calls and résumés	Optimism
6	More phone calls	Discouragement, anger, resentment
7	Broadcast letters	Depression, withdrawal
8	Think about starting business	Hope and discouragement
9	Systematize job search	Grieving and letting go
10	Second-round calls to contacts	Determination
11	Referrals increase	Self-esteem improves
12	First-round interviews	Excitement
13	Waiting for callbacks	Doubt, anxiety
14	Renewed phone calls	Determination
15	Increased use of phone	Pride
16	Second-round interviews	Confidence
17	Job offer received	Excitement, doubt, confusion
18	Job offer evaluation	Cautious optimism
19	Decline first job offer	Doubt, remorse
20	Renewed job search	Renewed determination
21	Four second-round interviews	Excitement
22	Three third-round interviews	Confidence
23	Three job offers	High
24	Job offer evaluation	Determination
25	Salary negotiation	Cautious and confident
26	Accept job offer	Excitement and concern about reentry

graveyard-shift customer service reps. "How do you fix this thing?" Jerry lay awake knowing that it was the last call he would take.

He got to work extra early that morning. His boss got in early, too, and called him into the office. "Jerry, I'm sorry. I feel crummy about this but today is your last day. Here is your layoff notice. You'll need to sign these waivers. Please clear out your office by noon today and leave all your file keys with me before you go. There is a three-day job

search workshop put on by an outplacement firm that begins tomorrow morning in Los Angeles. Be on the plane this afternoon."
"But I need some time to clear out my things and tell my wife and. . .."
"I know it's rushed, but this workshop is scheduled for tomorrow, and if you don't show up you'll miss out."

Jerry called his wife and told her the news, then cleaned out his office and was home by noon. He was numb. His wife was outraged, frustrated, upset, and helpless to change anything. She had been part of the company, too. Then Jerry left for the three-day workshop.

The workshop leader met with twelve employees, all axed the day before, in the hotel across from the career transition firm's office. The leader started off by welcoming them to the job search class and telling them, "Your only job now is to get another job." Three hours later, the group finished venting their anger. They were angry at Unisys. They felt betrayed. Let down. These were strong emotions from loyal employees. Once the initial venting of emotions passed, the next two and a half days were productive and interesting. The displaced employees focused on identifying their values and interests, assessing their skills, and writing down their accomplishments. They were given tips on the job search process and instructed in interviewing techniques and salary negotiations. By the end of the session, each had produced a résumé and had a list of networking contacts to call.

So Jerry sat for a couple of weeks. He ran a few errands and started fixing dinner in the evenings, but mostly he sat and thought about things. He thought about what he would really like to do. After a couple of months, he went to a nearby job club and tried out one or two other local resources. His former boss called him a couple of times and apologized again and again. "If only I hadn't persuaded you to take this new job, then maybe you would still be working." He sure felt bad about it. Jerry occasionally talked to his former staff and colleagues. Two bosses were now doing the work of three. They had thirty employees to supervise instead of ten to fifteen. And people seemed a little worried about what would happen to them and to their jobs. How come they weren't fired? Was it just a matter of time? Should they keep their heads down and just keep plugging away? Should they start job hunting on their own time?

Jerry got a call from a headhunter. The opportunity sounded great. He went in for the interview, but it wasn't the job he had been led to believe it would be. Some other friends called and invited him to come down and take a look at a job that had opened in another branch of Unisys. He had been out of work for ten weeks. The severance pay would last until August. According to the rules of the company, if he were formally offered another position at Unisys and didn't accept, his severance pay could be terminated. But the offer was informal for the moment. So he went down and looked it over. Then he took it.

After a month on the job, he knew it was the wrong one for him. So when the next round of layoffs began in June, he volunteered to be fired again. This time he and his wife took a vacation; he spent time fixing things; he helped his mother move into his brother's home; and he thought seriously about what he would really like to do.

He had heard about an all-volunteer job club sponsored by the state employment agency. He signed up and started volunteering and sending out the word that he was looking for a new position. A notice appeared on the board for a sales representative manager for an airline parts firm—one that was doing well in sales and had a small working staff. It had all the elements of a job that he liked: a lot of responsibility, a chance to make a difference, a small-sized firm with a lot of potential, and good management. He interviewed, and, two weeks later, he started work. Now, a year later, he knows he made the right decision.

As he looked back on the first layoff, he acknowledged that he was depressed and unable to function for the first couple of months. The career transition workshop was helpful, but he couldn't put it to use just then. It wasn't until six months later that he could really go over the workshop material and turn it into reality. He took a quick-fix job but that didn't work. His wife was still angry at Unisys—and maybe he was, too. Now when he talks to his old friends at the old job, they're not so sure that he didn't get the better deal by being fired.

How Long Will It Take?

The first thing client companies and candidates ask is, "How long will it take to find a new job?" The general answer that used to roll off every career transition firm's collective tongue was, "One month for every $10,000 in salary." However, if the candidate is in the $100,000+ range and wants to locate in an area where there are few jobs, it will take longer. Similarly, people with job skills that are in high demand will find it easier to move into their new position. With the number of employee terminations remaining at a steady high level, the length of time to find new employment is increasing. Lee Hecht Harrison, an international career management firm, says that in 1993 finding a new position took nearly six months.

The Association of Outplacement Consulting Firms International (AOCFI) conducted a survey of their member firms in October of 1990. One finding was that 21 percent of those being outplaced had more than eleven years tenure in their last job; the average age of all job seeking candidates was 42.2 years—a little older for women.

How can companies ease the transition for their employees and move them more quickly into their new positions? One of the most common solutions is to provide career transition services.

CAREER SERVICES AVAILABLE TO EMPLOYEES

There are an enormous number of services that a company can provide in-house or through outsourcing that will help their ex-employees more quickly find their next jobs. Part of the challenge is to identify what the services are and which ones fit the needs of the ex-employees and the company. Picture a cube with all of the available services listed in a vertical column (see illustration 7). The horizontal row includes the kinds of employees who are being discharged— executive/managers, professionals, hourly workers, workers with special needs, and so on. The third dimension of the cube includes the organizations that can provide the services, meaning career transition firms, Private Industry Councils, unions, and nonprofit agencies. A description of their services is in this chapter and in chapter 7.

Three typical kinds of candidates and the services that are commonly provided to them following outplacement are described in table 5. Fuller descriptions of the services are listed alphabetically at the end of the chapter.

How Do I Determine Which Services to Use and Who Will Provide Them?

Each downsizing organization needs to determine by category of employee the mix of services that best meets exiting employee needs. See the "Checklist for Services for Exiting Employees" for determining which services to use.

The style and manner in which an organization manages its exiting employees is indicative of its values and operating style. Sun

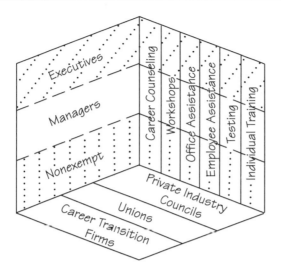

Illustration 7 Identifying Services That Fit Employee and Company Needs

Microsystems gave their employees—computer technicians, warehouse employees, clerical and accounting staff—four to six months notice. Employees were disappointed to leave the company, wanted to continue working, and sought to prove how valuable they were by increasing their production level. During a career self-reliance course, they sought to help each other out and spoke well of the company and its management. At another company, employees were told to be out within the hour and to show up the next day for a training session. Not surprisingly, employees vented their anger against the company, against their management, against the product, and to the customers. When the company starts hiring again, predictably they'll find it harder to recruit good employees. The word is out.

Kinds of Career Transition Services

So what are the services that contribute to a displaced executive's, professional's, or hourly worker's successful job campaign? The career transition firm's services and fees are changing dramatically. Throughout the 1980s, career transition /outplacement firms charged

Table 5 Services Typically Provided to Employees

Outplacement Services	Executive	Manager/ Professional	Hourly/ Nonexempt
Private office	X		
Secretarial support	X		
Health club membership	optional		
Employee assistance program: drug/alcohol/family	X	X	X
Support group	X	X	
Computer broadcast résumé			X
Postage and office supplies	X		
Answering service	X		
Telephones	X	X	
Psychological services	X	X	
Career assessment	X	X	X
Résumé writing	X	X	X
Indiv. training: résumé writing	X	X	X
Indiv. training: interviewing skills	X	X	X
Indiv. training: telephone skills	X	X	
Indiv. training: job search	X	X	X
Indiv. training: salary negotiation	X	X	
Business plan evaluation	X		
Spousal counseling	X	X	
Unlimited time in process	X		
3- to 6-month outplacement services	X	X	X
1- to 3-day training and services		X	X
1- to 6-hour indiv. counseling		X	
Job clubs		X	X
Group training: résumé writing		X	X
Group training: interviewing skills		X	X
Group training: telephone skills		X	X
Group training: job search strategies		X	X
Group advice: dress and etiquette		X	X
Group training: multilanguage			X
Self-study resources		X	X
Membership in local career center	X	X	X
Job fairs		X	X
Résumé distribution	X	X	X
Clipping service	X	X	
Library	X	X	optional
Computer	X	X	
Access to job postings	X	X	X
Getting community assistance		X	X
Using federal/state/county assistance programs			X
Unemployment/welfare			X

Checklist of Services for Exiting Employees

❑ Who will we provide services for?

- Executives

- Middle managers and professionals

- Hourly staff

- Employees with special needs

❑ What kinds of services will be provided?

- See list at end of chapter

❑ What are the monetary costs?

- In-house

- External career transition firm

- Private Industry Council

- Community services

❑ What quality of services will be provided?

- Develop in-house capabilities (time, cost, volume, and availability issues)

- External resources—single source/multiple sources

- Combination of internal and external resources

❑ What are time and availability considerations?

- When are the services needed (e.g., tomorrow)

- For how long?

a percentage, usually 12 to 15 percent, for the services they provided an executive or middle manager, plus an administrative fee. In the 1990s, with the rapid increase in the number of career transition firms and independent career transition consultants, there is currently an unbundling of services. Now companies can contract for any combination of services and specify the length of time an ex-employee can receive them. Internal career centers frequently outsource some services—for example, one-on-one job search strategy coaching for senior executives, psychological counseling, and entrepreneurial workshops.

TYPICAL CAREER TRANSITION SERVICES

The following are four typical categories of career transition services. They are described according to (a) user profile, (b) structure, (c) location, (d) staffing, (e) time limit, (f) company feedback, (g) fee structure, and (h) services. Each of the variations satisfies different needs. The challenge is to fit these services to the needs of the organization and the exiting employees.

Executive Career Transition Services

Executive career transition services were the earliest established outplacement services. They are called by various names: *full service outplacement, executive outplacement,* or *complete package outplacement.* Whatever the name, they are the most extensive, complex, demanding, and costly of the career transition services.

Profile of candidates. The program is designed for executives, senior managers, or highly paid professionals who earn more than $60,000 per year. Some companies use $80,000 per year as the cutoff point. Others reserve this service for employees at the director level and above. Others specify a pay range, such as level 23 and above.

Structure. Executive career transition services are always provided on a one-on-one basis. Small groups might be formed for specific training objectives, support, and networking.

Location. The executive candidate's new office is located at the career transition firm or at the executive suite of the in-house career center. Career transition firms are located in the heart of the business district in order to be close to the action, or located close to the company's offices, or even located in the suburbs close to where many of the candidates live. Candidates use an individual room on a first-come–first-served basis or by signing up for the times they know they will be in the new office. Frequently, the office is a comfortable cubicle with a desk, chair, phone, and office supplies.

Staffing. The candidate's counselor is an experienced career transition consultant who knows the business community. In addition, there may be a psychologist on staff or at least available on a consulting basis. Sometimes additional counselors and trainers will be made available for group or individual coaching on specific job search skills or broad issues such as financial or business planning.

Time limit.   Historically, there has been no limit on the time that the career transition firm or consultant will spend with the candidate. Some executive career transition firms and in-house centers are now offering optional time-limited contracts for a defined period of time, for example, six, nine, or twelve months. This trend is accelerating in the 1990s.

Client company feedback.   The outplacement firm's counselors write or phone regular feedback reports on a predetermined schedule negotiated with the client company. Some companies want time-oriented reports (e.g., once a month); others want information after each phase (e.g., after orientation, after assessment, after training). An example of a feedback letter is given in figure 9.

Fee structure.   The traditional fee for executive outplacement is 15 percent of gross annual compensation for the previous year. According to Kennedy Publications, in their 1990 *Analysis of the Outplacement Consulting Business in North America,* 40 percent of the 226 companies listed as outplacement firms charged 15 percent of salary. The reported range is from 5 percent to 25 percent. About 69 percent of the firms have a minimum average fee of $3,000 to $5,000. Only 13 percent report a minimum salary level, generally grouped in the $30,000 to $40,000 range.

One of the more controversial issues is the desire of some companies and some individuals to negotiate to receive a fixed dollar amount in lieu of transition services. The Internal Revenue Service issued Revenue Ruling 92-69 in September 1992, which deals with this issue.

Services.   At the beginning of this chapter, we left Steve Moir, the former senior vice president for sales, surprised and shaken by the news of his termination from the manufacturing firm. What happened to him next? What services could the outplacement firm provide him?

In the next room, waiting for Steve, was Ray Morse, the career transition professional who was to be his counselor throughout the job search process. During the intake interview, Ray talked to Steve about the layoff

---

MORSE
Outplacement

Personal and Confidential

June 30, 1994

Stuart Aubret, President and CEO
Streeter-Haaz Corporation
1234 Research Parkway
Marton, NJ

Dear Stuart:

This letter is to give you an update on the progress of Rosa Romera, who we have been working with since May 19, 1994.

Rosa is progressing well and has completed the following elements:

- Skills and interest inventory
- Development of a clear and realistic goal
- Résumé writing

Rosa is currently working on the following goals:

- Development of a self-marketing plan
- Development of a contact network

I will keep you posted on Rosa's progress. She and I would both appreciate any referrals and suggestions that you may make.

Sincerely,

Ray Morse

Ray Morse
Morse Outplacement

Figure 9   Feedback Letter to the Client Company

and how he felt about it. If there was any concern that Steve was not handling the layoff well, that he was suicidal (very rare) or terribly emotional, Ray would stay with him until he had stabilized. Ray talked to Steve about what he might say to his family, subordinates, religious leader, clubs, colleagues and friends, helping him work through any barriers he might have in conveying the news. Steve had already received a written letter stating the severance and benefits information.

It would take a day or two before he could really understand what it said. The counselor volunteered to help Steve clean out his office later that evening after taking him to the career transition center for a brief orientation and to show him the structured support available there for the next phase of his life. Within a day or two, Steve arrived at the career transition center and began a new job—the job of finding a job.

The full range of services a candidate might receive include:

- Initial intake interview
- Opportunity to vent feelings
- One-on-one counseling
- Individual assessment
- Individual coaching
- Psychological testing
- Résumé writing assistance
- Résumé printing
- Phone training
- Financial planning advice
- Goal setting
- Job search strategy
- Salary negotiation training and advice
- Support group
- Business plan evaluation
- Family counseling
- Dress and etiquette training and advice
- Office support
- Library use
- Computer use
- A desk, phone, desk supplies
- Phone answering service or message center
- Mailing résumés
- Interview training
- Spousal counseling

- Support of fellow colleagues
- Job postings from executive and senior level search services

The descriptions of these services are at the end of this chapter.

And so those outplaced began the next phase of their life. Many people, particularly those used to a routine, find that going to an office on a regular schedule is the most productive way to successfully find a new job. Some prefer "going to work" every day from 8 A.M. to 1:00 P.M. Other candidates who may have short-term family commitments and a strong networking base may prefer being in the "office" on Tuesdays, Wednesdays, and Thursdays from 9:00 A.M. to 3:00 P.M. Others put in twelve-hour days each day and conduct their personal business on the weekend. The incentive for the candidates to maintain regular hours is the increased likelihood of moving more quickly into their next position. Some have been under such incredible strain that they need a break or need to take care of pressing family business before they can spend full time in the job search process.

What happens to the executive clients when they arrive at their new office at the career transition firm? If appropriate, they are given a series of personality and skill assessments that help them stabilize their self-worth and revitalize their self-image. Then the firm works with them to write their résumés, to focus in on the kind of job they want to pursue, to help develop leads for informational interviews, and to assist in developing an extensive network of contacts. Usually this takes place in the first two to three weeks. During the rest of the first month, executives are coached in telephone, interviewing, and salary negotiation skills. Throughout the process, the candidates meet with their counselors to review progress, find new leads, and stay motivated. Rejection is difficult for everyone and particularly for those seeking new positions. The support of the counselor and the shared camaraderie with other executive candidates help maintain the motivation and perseverance during the time it takes to find the next position.

Professional and Midlevel Manager
Career Transition Services

What kinds of services are provided to middle managers and midlevel professionals? Generally, group services with the addition of some individual services are provided. In-house career centers generally offer a few more one-on-one sessions.

Profile of candidates. These group programs are designed for nonexempt employees and mid to lower level managers and professionals. The salary level will vary considerably by regions.

Structure. Candidates are placed in groups of ten to fifteen people and given one to three days training. At the close of the program, candidates are often on their own; there may be no follow-up by the company nor additional services provided. Some companies provide two to ten individual follow-up meetings and print fifty résumés. Candidates continue their job search out of their home or through a nonprofit job search organization's facilities. In-house career services frequently provide support groups, cubicles on a space-available basis, and ongoing topical workshops. Some companies provide a list of career, career transition, and networking resources within the community.

Location. The training is held away from the company—sometimes in the career transition firm's training facility, sometimes at a nearby hotel.

Staffing. Career transition consultants, professionally trained in-house career counselors or human resource staff, or trainers from public or nonprofit organizations staff the courses.

Time limit. Usually candidates receive services just for the time that they are in the class. Sometimes, two to ten individual follow-up sessions are spread over the next four to six weeks. In-house services are usually offered for three to twelve months following termination and are similar to the executive services.

Client company feedback. Feedback is provided on the number of people who attended the training and the kinds of issues that were raised that might affect the company.

Fee structure. A dollar amount is charged per person ($100 to $250 per person per day), or $1,500 to $2,500 is charged per training day for each trainer, with a maximum group size of twenty people.

Services. Training content might include the following:
- Group ventilation of feelings associated with job loss
- Identification of career values, interests, and style
- Identification of skills
- Training in identifying a network of contacts
- Establishment of new goals
- Training in résumé writing and interviewing

- Training in phone skills, dress, and etiquette
- Help in identifying potential employers
- Help in getting assistance from the community
- Generalized personal financial planning advice
- Training in salary negotiation
- Optional: résumé writing service

Hourly Employee Career Transition Services

Profile of candidates.   In-house or external programs are conducted for the lower level employee who is nonexempt and earning less than $30,000 per year (regional variations will affect the average salary). Not infrequently, candidates will speak English as a second language and will have strong cultural ties.

Structure.   A transition center sometimes is provided for self-help. There are also group training sessions, ranging in length from one-half day to three days, which focus on specific topics such as completing the application form or résumé writing, or which cover some of the same range of material used for middle managers.

Location.   The transition center is usually located away from the mainstream of the company's activities, and in some cases may be located off-site.

Staffing.   The company's human resource professionals and/or career counselors can coordinate the process and manage the transition center or an external agency can be brought in to provide the initial training. Sometimes, in lengthy or large layoffs, a career transition firm counselor or private industry council job search rapid response team is stationed at the company to provide consultation for workers and management services for company officials.

Time limit.   The services last as long as the layoffs continue and generally not more than six months after the last layoff.

Client company feedback.   Feedback is provided on the number of people who attend the training, the number who visit the transition center, and the kinds of issues that are raised that might affect the company.

Fee structure.   Career transition firms will usually contract for $1,500 to $2,500 per day per trainer for training a group of ten to twenty-five people. For $300 to $400 per day, the organization can contract for one consultant to manage the transition center.

Services. Services provided at the transition center may include the following:

- Phones
- Desk space
- Library of reference books
- Job listings from local companies
- Support groups, job clubs
- Information on how to apply for unemployment or welfare services
- Help in getting assistance from various community resources
- Personal computers
- Job search counselors
- Résumé printing assistance

Training content. Training content is similar to that provided for the midlevel managers and professionals:

- Group ventilation
- Résumé writing
- Completing application forms
- Developing a contact network
- Assessment (values, interests, goals)
- Interviewing skills
- Phone skills, dress, and etiquette
- Salary negotiation
- Skill identification
- Job search skills

VARIATIONS ON CAREER TRANSITION SERVICES

Every company needs to tailor its termination procedures to fit its needs and the needs of its employees and the community in which they live and work. Some companies have unique needs, for example, they are located in remote, single-company towns or in high unemployment areas. Some have hired workers who speak languages other than English and need translation services. Companies need to consider the special needs of older workers, minorities, and those with disabilities.

Most career transition firms work closely with companies to craft a program to meet the needs of their exiting employees and the company's desired end results. The themes and variations of services provided are endless. Factors that influence the final design and contract of the career transition support services include quality, cost, and volume of services needed, capability and availability of internal and external resources, and insightfulness regarding the best way to help ex-employees quickly get back into the workforce.

CAREER TRANSITION REFERRAL RESOURCES FOR EXITING EMPLOYEES

The agencies listed in the checklist below should be contacted to find out how they can help and the following information should be gathered for each:

- Agency
- Address
- Phone number (including any toll-free numbers)
- Hours of service
- Description of the kinds of service they provide

Checklist of Referral Resources

❑ In-house career transition resources
  - Career transition center
  - Career transition staff
  - Employee assistance program: stress assistance, personal counseling
  - Benefits office: health and retirement information
  - Continuing education services

❑ Community career transition resources
  - Private Industry Counsel (PIC) and/or job training program (JPTA) office
  - Employee Development Department employment and/or training offices
  - Unemployment office
  - Local branches of nonprofit agencies with career transition or job club programs
  - Forty Plus, Operation ABLE, YMCA/YWCA, other nonprofit agencies

- Chamber of commerce
- Career centers
- Union career transition programs
- Private career counselors, career counseling firms, outplacement/ career transition firms who accept self-paying clients
- Permanent and temporary employment agency firms
- Legal aid societies
- Financial aid services
- Adult school and college programs
- Admissions or counselor's office (includes kinds of academic, certificate, and training programs available; also include financial aid information)
- Academic career centers (identify their clientele and the kinds of resources available to nonstudents, students, and alumni)
  - Literacy programs
  - English as a second language programs
- Counseling programs
  - Alcoholics Anonymous and Al-Anon
  - Drug treatment centers
  - Women's shelter programs
  - Crisis counseling
  - Centers, hospitals, hotlines, counselors
- Special service agencies (particularly if they have career transition programs)
  - Disabled
  - Older worker
- Cultural organizations (Hispanic, Asian, etc.)
- Religious organizations (Jewish, Latter-Day Saints, etc.)
- Other local resources

DESCRIPTIONS OF SERVICES: AN ALPHABETICAL GLOSSARY OF TERMS

Definitions and descriptions of the services that might be provided to executives, middle managers, first-line supervisors, hourly employees, and blue collar staff are given below.

Benefits. All employees need information about the continuation of health plans, COBRA, retirement programs, and pretax-dollar investment programs for themselves and their families. This should be prepared in written form and given to each exiting employee.

A generalized statement also needs to be given to the ongoing strategic workforce so they will know how their former colleagues are being treated and what they might expect in future downsizings.

Business plan evaluation.   One of the options candidates from all levels sometimes want to explore is the opportunity to go into business for themselves. There are several sources that have developed a specialty of helping candidates create a business plan and assisting them in evaluating its potential for success. Sources include transition firms, financial planners, accountants, the local chamber of commerce, and federal and state agencies.   Several career transition firms routinely make this service available to their executive candidates who are receiving one-on-one assistance.

Career assessment and goals.   Assessment instruments give the candidates information about personality styles, vocational interests, and values. The *Myers-Briggs Type Indicator®* instrument, *Strong Interest Inventory,® Motivated Skills Card Sort, FIRO-B, 16 PF, Career Design Guide,* and *Career Values Card Sort* are among the more commonly used. There are numerous other instruments that assess additional psychological factors.

During the assessment phase, candidates examine their career and life values, interests and achievements, and skills and competencies. They analyze the kinds of successes they have had and seek a pattern of achievement. This will form the basis of their career objective on their résumé. Candidates have the unique opportunity to revisit their career dreams and goals. For many, once they have gotten over the shock of being laid off, they feel exhilarated and even rejuvenated. They have a second chance to rethink their dream of being a firefighter or to sail around the world or to be successful once more in their current field.

Clipping service.   National organizations are in the business of seeking and clipping job positions by function and selling them. Sometimes these are made available in hard copy, sometimes through computer on-line systems.

Community assistance.   Community assistance takes several forms:

- Job service transition programs
- Economic assistance resources
- Psychological services for individuals and families

It is essential that the downsizing organization provide staff for in-house employee assistance programs or contract with community

agencies or private firms to provide personal, crisis, family, rehabilitation, and alcohol and substance abuse services for their exiting employees. There is commonly a dramatic increase in family
violence and substance abuse as a result of the loss of a job.

Company car. As long as the employee is on the company payroll,
some organizations will allow the executive to use the car during
executive job searches.

Counseling for the candidate. This can take a wide range of approaches. Occasionally the candidate has drug or alcohol problems
that need to be addressed. Sometimes the marriage and family begin to fall apart because of the additional stress of being out of work.
Emotional problems or problems with a wide variety of interper-
sonal relationships can surface on or off the job. Not everyone needs
this service; however, every major job transition organization (private, nonprofit, and public) either has a psychologist on staff or
can bring in a consultant to offer guidance and direction to the
candidate and the firm.

Many candidates are physically and emotionally exhausted. They
want to sleep, to take some time to rest, and to let their bodies and
spirit recover. Some have personal obligations that have been put
on hold, such as repairing their car, settling a parent's estate, or
completing projects for clubs or other outside organizations. It is
up to the counselor and the candidate to decide how much time
the candidate needs to rest and how soon he or she will need to
move into the next phase.

Counseling for family members. Sometimes a member of a
candidate's family becomes so distressed with the loss of the job
that it would be useful to provide marriage, family, or child counseling. This is true for all levels of transition candidates. The service can be provided by the career transition firm, private counselors that the company contracts with, or social service agencies
within the community.

Counseling for the candidate's spouse. A candidate's spouse may
also need counseling assistance. For many candidates, particularly
business executives, senior public officials, and military officers,
spouses are part of the business and part of the job. They were interviewed at the start of the job and they were expected to contribute to their spouse's success. The loss of a job affects their lives as
well.

Dress and etiquette training and coaching. Many candidates need advice on what is appropriate and inappropriate to wear to a job interview. Those whose informational and more formal interviews include breakfast, lunch, and dinner meetings can occasionally benefit from etiquette coaching.

Employee assistance programs. Individuals under stress have a greater propensity for drug, alcohol, and family abuse. The availability of these programs on a one-on-one or group basis or through the community service agencies is essential.

Financial planning. In-house or external transition organizations sometimes contract with financial planners to assist their senior and midlevel managers with estate and retirement planning as well as debt reduction assessment and implementation planning. Blue collar and lower level employees can also benefit from this assistance.

Grief counseling. All candidates can be expected to go through the predictable stages of emotions associated with losing their job or career. These stages include shock, immobilization, disbelief, anger, bargaining, frustration, and, finally, grieving. It is critical that candidates surface and deal with all of these emotions in order to get on with the job search. If denied, the candidates tend to get stuck and unable to move successfully into their next position.

Individual image coaching. Occasionally, candidates need to be coached to improve their physical appearance, lose weight, or improve their personal hygiene. This is part of the ongoing process to encourage, motivate and help the candidate to move into a new career position.

Intake interview. The intake interview is conducted by transition counselors, welfare workers, or unemployment services to assess the current and future needs of their clients. The following are common examples of intake interviews:

- A manager turns over a recently terminated candidate to a career transition counselor who is waiting in the next room. During the intake interview, or "pick-up," the counselor assesses the candidate's emotional reactions and plans for the next steps.

- The out-of-work blue collar employee meets with the PIC or union counselor who determines the person's eligibility for local, state, and federally funded career assessment and training programs.

- The transition counselor assesses the financial and emotional stage the candidate is in and plans for the next appropriate steps (normal stages include ventilation, psychological readiness to move forward, career assessment, career exploration, career strategy for finding the next position, evaluation of options).

Interests. As part of the assessment phase, candidates identify their interests—those subjects and activities that grab their attention. Frequently, identifying interests can lead to developing them as a profession or as an avocation.

Interview training. Candidates are coached on what is appropriate and inappropriate to wear to an interview and how to answer the tough questions like, Why did you leave your last job? How come you've been out of work for a while? They're also taught how to ask questions and what kind of information to seek. They learn to structure the interview session so that it can be advantageous to them and to the interviewer. One of the more useful technologies is to use the video camera to tape practice interview sessions.

Job fairs. Prospective employers are invited by the downsizing organization to set up booths and to interview exiting employees. These corporate sponsored job fairs are similar to the ones held at college campuses and by communities.

Job postings/job listings. One of the first tasks of a career center is to get on the mailing lists of all the local companies to receive their job postings. Career transition firms, nonprofit agencies, and all job service organizations routinely receive job postings. Another major service provided by substantial organizations is hard copy and/or computerized on-line listings of all in-house posted positions. (An issue to be resolved in-house is the priority order of who will fill those positions: the continuing workforce, the exiting workforce, or external job seekers.)

Job search strategy. One of the greatest strengths of transition coaching is its ability to help clients develop and maintain a job search strategy. Job search strategy has two forms:

- Initial strategy includes writing a résumé, planning and conducting informational interviews, going on formal interviews, and negotiating for salary and benefits.
- Long-term strategy includes planning how to sustain personal energy and vitality over a period of several months.

It is easy for candidates at all levels to become discouraged about their job search after a month or two goes by without a job interview. A strategy that reinforces the job search process is essential to success. Career transition organizations tend to emphasize this phase of the campaign. They develop simple and sophisticated tracking systems, reports, and feedback processes and plan celebrations and joyful occasions that encourage job seekers to persevere over a potentially lengthy search.

Library.   Directories, job postings from local companies, national job referral and search services, references on company information, phone books, catalogs of useful search resources, and local and national newspapers are common staples of libraries. These resources are standard offerings in outplacement firms and in-house transition services. Most community colleges, public libraries, and private industry council job centers also house these important references.

Mailing computerized targeted letters.   Some job seekers and job assistance organizations send out a large number of individual résumés to companies in the hope of receiving a few requests for interviews. Career transition firms, unions, and nonprofit job search firms will occasionally provide assistance in broadcast mailings of large numbers of résumés for a candidate. While the strategy is not as successful as networking, it is one of the possible strategies to use in a job search.

Membership in local career centers.   Community centers exist in many regions that provide an alternative source of job search counsel. Corporations and organizations hold memberships for themselves and make them available to their exiting employees for a defined period of time, usually one year.

Multilanguages.   With the increasing internationalization of the workforce, group training services sometimes need to be conducted in the candidate's home language.

Networking.   This is the most important element of the job search process. Networking involves identifying and then contacting friends, colleagues, family, religious contacts, former bosses and subordinates, and neighbors to talk to them about the desired position and to develop leads about possible job openings. Research indicates that two-thirds of all jobs are found through networking—at all levels of employment and for all occupations. This is a skill and an attitude that can be learned.

Office, phone, desk supplies.   This is typically available to the executive and midlevel candidate. The office is usually a small office or cubicle located close to the firm's library and to other candidates. The phone is the lifeblood of the job campaign and an essential piece of equipment for successfully finding a job. The national nonprofit agencies and some of the PIC programs also make phone services available to their clients.

Office support.   Most senior managers are used to having secretarial and other support services to assist them with their phone calls, letters, and other office functions. Executive outplacement firms can provide them with these additional services as needed.

Phone skills training.   Candidates need information on how to make cold calls, how to respond to advertisements, how to call for informational interviews, and how to most effectively use the telephone to market themselves. Some candidates also need guidance on how to speak clearly and with the appropriate volume and tone of voice.

Psychological support.   Crisis lines, 24-hour hot lines, and similar services to assist those in distress are an important adjunct to all exiting employees and those who are continuing as part of the strategic workforce.

Receptionist and phone answering services.   The telephone is the crucial communication device for job seekers. A separate or tagged line is commonly available for senior-level candidates, which can be answered by the receptionist as if it were the candidate's office. Some career transition firms and in-house transition centers offer individual voice-mail services. Transition centers also typically offer a message center with a receptionist.

Reports to the downsizing organization.   Progress reports on the candidate are commonly requested by the downsizing organization. See figure 9 on page 146 for a typical example.

There are several issues in the outplacement industry regarding these reports.

- The career transition firms and agencies want to hold their candidates accountable for progress, they want to show their client company that the firm is successful (i.e., helping the candidate progress toward getting a new job), and they don't want the candidate or themselves to be forgotten by the company (the out-of-sight–out-of-mind syndrome). If everything is going well, the reports are easy to write. If not, then in how many ways can the firm write that "the candidate is making slow but steady progress"?

- The company wants to hold both the candidate and the job transition service accountable. Some want only verbal reports; others want it in writing.

- The candidate wants the report to be accurate, fair, and supportive. The worst report is one that is punitive and blames the candidate unfairly.

The reports build trust between the client company and the job transition service, between the service and the candidate, and even between the client company and the candidate. Their accuracy and fairness is important from all perspectives. To promote trust between candidate and consultant, it is important that personal information such as test results not be included in the report.

Confidentiality is another major consideration. Frequently, candidates vent their frustration, anger, remorse, and fears to their counselors. These conversations should not be reported back to the company. This venting and working through the emotions of severance from the organization is one of the main reasons that external career transition firms are used. It is part of the healing process. To report it back to the organization would be a violation of the counselor-candidate trust. As with all the counseling sessions, only situations that might endanger the client company or the individual should be reported—and then the candidates should be told that the threat is being taken seriously and will be acted on.

From the corporate viewpoint, the best reports are ones that are negotiated ahead of time. Usually transition services have standard formats and content. If the company has agreed to pay for particular services (e.g., testing of skills and abilities, résumé writing), the date that those services are completed should be on the report. Few client companies want to see the results of the tests and the training; they just want to know that it has been done. Client companies also want to know if there are any problems, such as the candidate disappearing, taking off on a two-month vacation, or refusing to write a résumé, or perhaps the candidate is planning on suing the company.

So, a simple little report suddenly begins to take on more importance. Some transition services show the outline of the reports to the candidates when they arrive so they'll know what to expect and what they are held accountable for. Some give copies of the completed reports to the candidates; some ask the candidates to provide input or to write the actual report; some hide the whole report. If the progress of the candidate is important to the company, the format of a progress report can be negotiated in the initial contract.

Résumé distribution. Downsizing companies gather the résumés of their departing employees and make them available or distribute them to other companies.

Résumé writing, résumé writing services. This is a standard feature in career and career transition services. The résumé is written to meet the needs of two people: the candidate and the new job interviewer. The candidate produces a résumé that clearly states the new career objective and therefore helps focus the career search. It also lists accomplishments and achievements over a lifetime, which gives a morale boost and a little extra oomph to the challenge of a job search. The résumé is, of course, valuable to the job screener and interviewer.

There is an incredibly large array of résumé writing books available in the marketplace. Executives generally have their résumés written jointly by themselves and their consultant and printed on high-quality paper. Middle managers have considerable assistance and frequently leave their three-day workshops with a printed résumé. Other candidates usually are offered guidance in group sessions, with an occasional brief one-on-one session to refine the product.

Sometimes companies arrange to print copies of a résumé and mail them for their ex-employees.

Salary negotiation training and advice. Senior and midlevel outplacement candidates usually receive information and advice on how to negotiate their salary offers. Middle managers get their information as part of their workshop (this is usually offered in three-day sessions). Executives can receive extensive one-on-one coaching.

Self-study resources. These include books, pamphlets, and videos describing phases of the job search process.

Setting goals. Once candidates have identified their skills, interests, and values and have explored the professions that can make use of their talents, they set goals. Goals can be part of the job strategy process (e.g., make thirty phone calls this week, set up two job interviews) or they can be part of their life strategy (e.g., get information about living in Alaska) or informational (what does an epidemiologist do?). Counselors encourage candidates to set and keep goals; it's an essential part of keeping the person active and in motion toward getting their next successful position.

Skill identification. This is part of the career assessment process. There are two basic kinds of skill identification: (a) self-identification of skills and competencies, and (b) actual assessment of skills performed (e.g., typing tests, data processing).

Special services. Special services are sometimes needed for the visually or hearing impaired or mentally or physically handicapped. Frequently, there are resources available in the community that can be contacted. Their services should also be listed in the resource guide.

Support groups, job clubs. All levels of ex-employees benefit from support groups—either formal or informal. They provide a morale boost, names for informational interviews, networking contacts, and motivation to keep working on the job of getting a job. Sometimes support groups are established by career transition firms; sometimes they are created within the community by nonprofit agencies or religious organizations. The oldest and strongest of the nationwide networking groups for executives and managers over the age of forty is Forty Plus.

Transition (career, resource) center. Transition centers are the hub or home base of the job-seeking candidate. They are a source of information and inspiration, a place of hope and despair.

The physical elements of a transition center include:

- A library for business magazines and specialized periodicals, newspapers, and reference books on organizations throughout the United States and the world
- A wallboard with job postings and listings from companies in the surrounding communities near the job site
- A copier to make copies of job postings, résumés, and company information
- A fax machine to send and receive information
- A kitchen area for coffee, tea, and soft drinks, with a refrigerator and microwave

- A training room and/or conference room
- Individual cubicles or shared working space
- Private counseling offices

Activities include:

- Counseling sessions
- Group training
- Constant phone calls
- Attending job fairs and scheduling onsite interviews (usually held in blue collar centers)

The psychological elements include:

- A businesslike atmosphere
- A convivial environment that encourages individuals but doesn't allow them to become too comfortable

Unemployment and welfare services. In large layoffs, companies and/or unions work with federal and state agencies to provide onsite information and referral services concerning unemployment, welfare, retraining, and employment services for their exiting employees. In smaller layoffs, this information is added to the list of career transition referral resources.

Values. Candidates who are newly out of a job frequently start thinking about what is important to them in their work life and their personal life. Frequently, the job transition time is a period of self-reflection about values. It is part of the assessment phase and contributes to the job search strategy process.

Ventilation: individual or group. Employees who have recently lost their jobs are usually frustrated and angry at the company and themselves. During the intake interview, the career transition consultant will talk to the executive candidate about the termination and how he or she feels about it. If there is any concern that the candidate is not handling the layoff well, the consultant will stay with the candidate until the emotions have stabilized.

In career workshops for middle managers and lower level staff, workshop leaders insist that during the first part of the session there will be a ventilation segment. Even if it is not scheduled into the session, the feelings will erupt during the meeting and will need to be addressed. While the angry and hurt feelings will come and go during the workshop and throughout the transition process, once the major ventilation has occurred, the participants will be able to move to the next phase of the process. Those who cannot release their feelings or who hope that the company will have a change of heart and call them back to work will probably not move as quickly forward into their next position.

It's generally nonproductive and not necessary for trainers and counselors to carry back the harsh words to the company.

9

Implementing
an Internal Career
Transition Center

After having met with Christina Perugia, Dr. Gene Smith, the training
and development manager, thought long and hard about the kinds of
services that the layoff required for Streeter-Haaz employees. Senior and
middle managers received individual and group outplacement services
from a private career transition firm. Some of the managers made use of
contacts within the executive recruiter ranks. Professionals used contacts
through trade and professional organizations. They also were given job
transition services. First-line supervisors were given extra job search help.
Hourly administrative and blue collar staff were provided with job search
and interviewing skills as well as lists of companies that were hiring.
Some of the unskilled workers or those with English as a second
language had a little more trouble and required additional help. All
employees received assistance with:

- Venting feelings and getting on with life
- Assessing current skill levels
- Reexamining career direction and goals
- Deciding what direction to take next
- Writing a résumé, cover letter, or application
- Learning where to find jobs
- Developing interviewing skills
- Obtaining unemployment benefits
- Maintaining morale

Some received information on:

- Financial planning
- Self-employment opportunities

Employers provided information that only their company could provide:

- COBRA health insurance benefits costs and procedures
- The status of their retirement plans
- What the company and individual supervisor would say when the prospective employer asked for a reference

Gene thought about the full spectrum of services designed to facilitate the layoffs at Streeter-Haaz. Then, thinking ahead, he wondered what a complete array of career services for Streeter-Haaz employees would look like.

For effective restructuring of the kind just described, four kinds of internal services meet both management requirements and employee needs:

- An in-house career transition service for exiting employees
- An inplacement service to relocate employees within the company as needed
- An ongoing career management program for the strategic workforce
- Organizational development services to help managers restructure and refocus their workforce

THE CAREER TRANSITION CENTER

An internal career transition center can be set up in downsizing organizations to meet management's requirements. In most cases, management will want to:

- Move staff quickly and smoothly into their new jobs—either within the company or externally
- Know that the process is fair and equitable
- Reduce or eliminate the number of grievances and lawsuits

Exiting employees have some of the same needs and some unique ones as well. In their career transition center, they will most likely want to:

- Move quickly and easily into new jobs that pay well, use their skills and abilities, and provide stability
- Regain their self-esteem
- Reduce the loss of financial and emotional security

A company sponsored in-house career center can meet all of these needs. There are several options. In-house career centers can be managed by in-house administrators or contracted out to external career transition organizations but located on-site. Another option is to send in-house candidates to an external transition firm's executive center or their multiple-client center. Some firms contract with other very large corporate centers to use their space for a defined time period (e.g., 3 months, 12 months) or contract with a local nonprofit agency to meet their needs on an ongoing basis.

The career transition center has several purposes, functioning as:

- An office to carry out the business of the job search
- A communications command post
- A psychological home base
- The home of a support group for the job seeker

Company Culture

The culture of the organization is conveyed through the style, tone, and services of the in-house transition center. Some question why anyone would want to pay so much attention to those who are exiting the company. Sometimes it serves to alleviate guilt. Sometimes it is for the more practical reason of quickly getting people back on payroll (someone else's payroll) and off company-paid unemployment. Sometimes it is also a statement from those who remain (i.e., the survivors who comprise the strategic workforce and are expected to meet current goals) that this company cares about its employees and wants to do well by them and that they will be well taken care of, too.

Cost

In-house centers are expensive to start up. They need space (rental, leased), furniture, computer equipment and software, phones and voice mail, file cabinets, private offices for counselors, open space offices for candidates, mail room facilities, copiers, fax machines, small kitchens (hot coffee and tea systems, cold drinks, maybe a refrigerator for lunches). Then there is the cost of library and job search services: local newspapers, the *Wall Street Journal,* the *National Business Employment Weekly,* local business publications, professional publications, and national business magazines. A very useful service is the computerized Dun and Bradstreet information and a computerized access to job postings. A 1-800 number is also useful. The cost needs to be weighed against the length of use (always longer than anticipated) and the availability of other resources.

Geographic Location

First, a few comments on some mistakes that companies have made in deciding where to establish career transition centers. "The boneyard" is often the name given to an out-of-the-way and maybe dilapidated surplus facility given over to displaced workers for their job search. Unfortunately, the stigma associated with such a facility prompts many job seekers to retreat to a solitary job search (or nonsearch) from home.

The facility should look like an office, a place where business is conducted. If the organization is outplacing managerial or white collar employees, don't choose a warehouse just because it is available. Managerial or white collar employees will not be comfortable going every day to such a setting to conduct a job search. In fact, they won't go to a nonprofessional office. Technical and blue collar workers also prefer a businesslike environment. If the company doesn't have an appropriate facility, it is a relatively minor expense to negotiate a short-term lease (say, four to six months) to an appropriately appointed and conveniently located facility.

Even in those cases where a company had adequate facilities for setting up a career transition center onsite, it might want to consider an off-site facility. One of the goals in termination is to assist the employee in making a clean break from the company. As long as the employee continues to feel like an employee, a lot of energy will be expended toward the organization. This energy can take the form of an unhealthy dependence on the company to "find me a job," or an uncomfortable anger and hostility toward the company that "used me up and threw me out!"

Some thought should be given to the geographic location of the facility. Look at the personnel records of the employees who will be leaving and plot their home addresses on a map. Then look at the local companies that most likely would need employees with the same skill mix as the employees that will be layed off. Plot the locations of these employees in a different color on the map. If the area is served by public transportation, superimpose the transit lines and terminal on the map. The ideal location will be (a) accessible to affected employees (i.e., it will be easy or convenient for them to come to work at the career transition center), (b) adjacent to the business community where the candidates will be applying for work, and (c) convenient to public transportation (with some level of economic insecurity, candidates may find public transportation more prudent than driving their own cars).

The Physical Facility

The career transition center must be large enough to permit the affected employees to conduct the business of reemployment. If the office is too cramped, the candidates will avoid coming to work; if it is too big, the candidates may feel lonely and alienated as though rattling around in a big old house. Candidates do not need their own private offices.

FURNISHINGS.   The following is a list of furnishings that are typical in the outplacement center.

Cubicles.   Small cubicles that allow private telephone conversations but lack the luxuriousness of private offices should be provided. If 100 employees are affected by the layoff, the transition center doesn't need 100 cubicles. Thirty or forty would more accurately reflect the number that would be used each day. During an active job search, candidates will spend only about one-third of their time on the telephone or writing letters. It is a common practice in the outplacement business to ask candidates to reserve cubicles a day or two in advance. Sometimes the scarcity of a commodity can drive up its demand. Signing up for a cubicle will also give the receptionist/office manager a rough estimate of when the job seeker will be in. This is particularly important when potential employers are responding to broadcast mailings or are calling back. Providing comfortable chairs is essential. The job seeker will be spending many hours on the telephone and writing letters—an uncomfortable situation for many that is greatly eased if they are sitting in comfortable, durable chairs.

Private offices. Senior managers, generally those making in excess of $100,000 per year, are frequently given a private or shared private office. The motivation here is to lessen the blow of being terminated from a high-level position. This type of office should have a high-back executive chair with a large wood executive desk, good art (or good reproductions) on the wall and, if available, a window. The distinguishing feature is that it is usually a shared office—several executives use the space at arranged times. Sometimes offices are designated; other times they are on a first-come–first-served basis by appointment.

Sign-in board. As in any office, it is critical that someone keep tabs on the whereabouts of the candidates. A sign-in/out or status board is essential. When potential employers call to speak to a candidate, the receptionist must be able to tell the caller exactly when the candidate will be in the office and/or can return the call.

Telephones. The single most critical tool in the career transition center is the telephone. The telephone is the conduit for instantaneous communication between candidate and potential employer. Each cubicle should be equipped with a telephone. If an older telephone system with eight to ten trunk lines and sixteen to twenty extensions are used, a receptionist should be available to answer incoming calls. Calls should be answered, "Executive office," or "Message center," since most candidates will not want prospective employers to know that they are contacting a transition center.

A more ideal configuration has a unique telephone number assigned to each candidate and a voice-mail system. The voice-mail system allows each candidate to answer the telephone when in the office (a common practice for today's managers and professionals), and to have the voice-mail answered with his or her own voice when not in the office. The candidate should be sure to include a voice-mail option of speaking with a "live person," in addition to leaving a recorded message. With voice mail, the candidate can use a unique code to retrieve telephone messages. The voice-mail option can give the transition candidate all the telephone communication power of an employed manager.

Fax machine.   The center should include at least one fax machine for prompt transmittal of résumés and cover letters to potential employers. The fax should be programmed to receive transmittals around the clock.

Computer support. Managers and professionals are computer literate, and the use of a computer is now an expected necessity in the workplace. The well-equipped transition center should contain several computers (both IBM PC compatibles and Macintoshes) and a letter-quality laser printer. The computer should be used not only by the clerical support staff but candidates should also be encouraged to draft letters and résumés on their own disks. Having résumés and standard cover and inquiry letters stored on the computer disk can facilitate the task of customizing each résumé to more closely match the job being recruited for. In addition, a computer spreadsheet or file system can greatly enhance the candidate's management of the job search process by keeping track of contacts and generating regular reports. A computer room can also include mailing lists of employers, headhunters, and venture capital firms for those candidates who opt to use broadcast and focused mass-mailing techniques.

Copy machines and mail room.   A good quality copy machine is essential, since candidates will need to keep copies of all outgoing correspondence for their files. Since slightly off-white stationery is preferred for résumés and correspondence, several types of stationery should be available in the copy room. The copy/mail room should also include a postage meter and an accurate scale.

Desk supplies.   Each cubicle should be equipped with standard supplies, including a wall calendar, stapler, paper clips, staple remover, scissors, ruler, self-stick removable notes, scratch paper, message pad, telephone book, and dictionary. But the desk in the cubicle should *not* contain a candidate's personal items or job search files. Each candidate should be assigned a locker or file cabinet drawer in which to store files when not in the cubicle conducting the job search. A central supply cabinet should be located near the file cabinets or lockers with legal pads, computer diskettes, staples, and other consumable supplies.

OFFICE CONFIGURATION.   The following office configuration is typical in career transition centers.

Receptionist area.   This is the central area of the career center. All candidates, counselors, and center managers keep people posted on their activities and location in this area. It should be located at the entrance and should be an attractive, inviting area that encourages people to ask questions and feel welcome.

Training room(s).   One of the most frequently used rooms in a transition center is the training room. Courses range from one-hour briefings to lengthy videotaped interviewing sessions to one-to-three day classes on job hunting skills. The training room should be located close to the coffee and beverage area yet in a separate space that will allow concentration and emotional venting in privacy.

An adequate site for clinics and networking meetings is an important part of the career transition center. The meeting room should be furnished with tables and comfortable chairs and should include a whiteboard, flip chart, and overhead projector. If the transition group is small enough, the tables can be configured in a U shape, providing maximum interaction between candidates. With a larger group, it may be necessary to place tables in schoolroom configuration.

Counselor offices.   Each counselor needs a private office to conduct one-on-one meetings with candidates. To ensure privacy, they should not be in open spaces or have see-through walls. Counselors need space to conduct venting and feedback sessions, report back to their clients on career inventory assessments, and hold updating meetings to encourage and support the continuing process of job search.

Library.   A reference library should be available to all candidates. It can be stocked with the following:

- Telephone directories
- *Directory of Directories*
- *The Encyclopedia of Associations*
- *Standard and Poor's Directory of Companies*
- Manufacturing association directories
- Chamber of commerce directories of business firms organized by Standard Industrial Classification (SIC) and coded for size of organization

The library could also contain books, audiotapes, and videotapes on job search skills, such as using the telephone, writing cover letters and résumés, networking, information interviewing, job interviewing, and salary negotiation. Directories of local and national executive search firms (headhunters) and venture capital firms might also be included.

Bulletin board area. There should be a candidate bulletin board located at a central point in the center, someplace where candidates will frequently congregate—possibly near the candidate message center. The topics and time of clinics and networking meetings should be displayed along with job leads that have been called into the transition center. The bulletin board can also list public job fairs, company open house notices, and upcoming visits to the transition center by company recruiters.

Video room. A video room should be equipped with a video recorder and monitor as well as a desk, three chairs, and a couch—furnishings that mirror an office that might be used for a job interview. When not being used to practice mock interviews (videotaped for later viewing or critiquing at home), the video room can be used to view personal development tapes.

Coffee break room. There should be a pot of coffee and a pot of hot water ready and waiting for candidates. This is a place to relax, to take a break, to meet other candidates and counselors, to exchange informal information, and to celebrate job landings. It should be easily accessible and easily managed (lots of coffee cups available, a refrigerator, and a designated person to keep it filled with supplies and cleaned up).

Candidate personal storage area. Many centers find it useful to have a separate, lockable, storage area for candidates to leave their personal supplies. It keeps the cubicles less cluttered and more easily accessible by multiple candidates and ensures the safety of personal items. If candidates care to be located in the center for a period of time, few will want to haul their special things back and forth from home to center to interview to class.

Staffing the Center

Center director. The center director is the administrator and the prime liaison between the company, the counselors, and the job seekers. This person needs to be able to manage a fluctuating budget and a fluctuating number of people in transition, market the services internally, work with external vendors, promote candidates to the external job world, and execute strong administrative skills. There are several sensitive situations that they must be able to handle:

- Staying close to the internal downsizing plans of the divisions and groups within the company
- Interfacing with internal managers who are facing discrimination charges from one of their discharged employees
- Working with exiting employees who are filing grievances or thinking about filing grievances and trying to conduct a job search at the same time
- Interacting with overeager managers who want too much information about their ex-employees
- Interacting with underresponsive managers who want to quickly move the candidates from their view, their mind, and their payroll
- Hiring and monitoring the quality of trainers and counselors
- Maintaining confidentiality

Counselor. This professional may be a member of the company's human resource staff, a consultant brought in from a career transition firm, or a specialist hired specifically for the short-term assignment. The counselor should have a private office and be available to candidates for both scheduled and emergency consultations. The counselor will not only provide one-on-one job search coaching, but might also lead technique clinics and candidate networking meetings. Some transition centers separate the responsibilities of the counselor and the trainer since they require different skills and abilities.

While there are few accreditation programs for counselors, the best known are the National Certified Counselor (NCC) and the National Certified Career Counselor (NCCC), which are sponsored by the National Board for Certified Counselors, Inc. The International Association of Outplacement Professionals also publishes a list of core competencies for career transition specialists.

Trainers. Trainers have two responsibilities: to teach job search skills and to motivate ex-employees to go through the job search process. They need to have a strong understanding of organizational expectations and need to be energetic, optimistic people. They don't need to be high-energy sales trainers, but they do need to be upbeat. Typically, trainers catch people at two stages: when they first receive their notification and they are either numb or angry, or later, when they need to refine their skills and restart a stalled career search.

Hiring contract trainers is a boom business for career transition organizations and centers. While word of mouth is a strong supplier of trainers, professional resources include the American Society of Training and Development, the National Society of Performance Instruction, the International Association for Outplacement Professionals, and Society for Human Resource Management. The International Association of Outplacement Professionals also includes guidelines for trainers in their list of core competencies.

Job developers.   Job developers have a tough job. Job seekers not only want them to find a job for them but are aggravated if postings aren't plentiful and available in their specific field. Job developers have a triple focus:

- Identify what kind of jobs will be sought by the incoming job seekers. This is frequently a guessing game and done on short notice. Meeting with individuals with special needs or meeting with small groups of job seekers with similar job focus usually works well.

- Find the local companies that provide those jobs (lists of companies provided by the Standard Industrialized Classification, the computerized Dun and Bradstreet, and the chamber of commerce are of major assistance) and get on mailing lists for job announcements from those firms.

- Educate job seekers on how to find jobs and how to find companies that might be likely job sources.

Psychologists and crisis counselors.   Many companies use their employee assistance program staff to provide crisis counseling services. It is useful to educate the employee assistance program staff on the unique needs of exiting employees and on how the company handles emergency and nonemergency situations. It is essential to have resources that can handle suicide prevention, substance abuse, family abuse, and depression. If there is a concern about personal security, then career center staff need to be apprised of how those sensitive issues will be handled.

While psychologists are expected to handle the more serious issues, they also provide the testing services for personality tests and other psychological inventories that might be used. Psychologists frequently are hired on a contract basis; in larger firms there might be a full-time professional on staff.

Benefits representative. While not officially part of the ongoing career center staff, benefits representatives will be called on frequently to explain severance, disability, medical, and sick leave benefits, retirement, vacation leave, COBRA, and other related questions. It is essential to have the information readily available and easily explainable to any exiting employee. If there are special arrangements or programs for departing employees, someone needs to be available at the other end of a phone line to answer questions. Once the stability and security of benefits is well understood, the job seeker can more readily get on with the job of finding a job.

Receptionist/office manager/clerical support. The receptionist is one of the key people in the career transition center. The receptionist knows when a candidate will be in the office, out on an interview, or available to return a call or reschedule a meeting. An upbeat, understanding, knowledgeable receptionist has a direct influence on the job seeker's responsiveness for the day's work.

Remote access counselor. A subcategory of counseling services is the availability of counselors via a 1-800 number or a regular charge number. Some centers have a home base in one location and provide a full range of career counseling services to staff who are located in a multistate territory via the telephone and fax machine. Some centers provide in-house training programs for their out-of-area job seekers and then provide follow-up via phone and fax. Others offer hot-line/job-line services. Remote access counselors need to attune themselves to voice inflections in addition to auditory cues of their clients.

Using Internal Staff Versus External Resources

As expected, there are advantages and disadvantages to using internal versus external counseling and training resources. Advantages of using internal staff include:

• Knowing the client base
• Knowing the culture

- Knowing how to access internal information
- Providing career opportunities for internal staff

Disadvantages of using internal staff include:

- Mistrust by clients
- Difficulty for an internal staff person to maintain confidentiality
- Possible awkwardness around venting of anger by job seekers against the internal person's friends, colleagues, and boss
- Occurrence of potentially compromising situations, such as knowledge of potential lawsuits or other actions by employees or being asked by the company to testify against an employee
- Difficulty for a counselor to maintain neutrality when helping a person leave a company (usually unwillingly) in which the staff member is still receiving rewards, promotions, and recognition
- Ineffective use of management time in a highly fluctuating work environment

Who Should the Career Transition Center Director Report To?

Human resource director.   HR is typically the functional organization that manages the career transition center, and the center director usually reports directly to the HR manager. Since the HR manager manages all of the personnel related functions, he or she can provide organizational support for the function. The human resource department usually knows about anticipated resizings and can keep the center director in the informational loop. If the HR function is not well respected, then the exiting employees will not be helped by the connection. Since resizing and terminating employees is generally a painful process, line managers will sometimes try to dump all the problems onto HR and walk away. However, they are the line managers and need to maintain a modicum of responsibility for their corporate shifts.

General manager.   Sometimes companies want the line managers to be directly responsible and responsive to their exiting employees, and therefore they create transition services that have in-department responsibilities. If all of the personnel services are decentralized, this can be a logical placement of the function.

Chief financial officer.   The chief financial officer is the one held accountable for the quantifying of the bottom-line numbers. If the downsizing/resizing is the result of trying to improve the bottom line, then occasionally the career center is also regarded as the CFO's responsibility.

The essential message to the company is that the exiting employees are being treated well and that those who are continuing the mission of the organization can rest assured that the company values their ongoing services and regrets having to divest itself of employees. Lean and mean approaches, no matter where the career center function reports, will produce lean and mean employees—and not necessarily highly productive ones.

Format of Services to Offer

Job search clinics.   An important aspect of the transition center is a regular series of technique clinics. These are group workshops where specific aspects of the job search are discussed and practiced. Clinics offer "how to" workshops in:

- Using the telephone
- Getting past the secretary
- Giving the correct response when asked, "Why did you leave your last job?"
- Responding to a blind ad
- Preparing a résumé
- Developing a network of contacts
- Keeping network contacts informed
- Mastering the job interview
- Handling the job offer
- Managing salary negotiations

The clinics serve not only to deal with the job search skills in question but also to bring the candidates together, promoting peer interactions and resulting in increased morale. An ideal time for the weekly clinic is on Monday morning. Job interviews are seldom scheduled on Monday mornings, and telephone calls are discouraged, as managers are trying to plan and organize the upcoming week while putting out fires from the past one. Having clinics on Monday mornings is also a good way to get all the candidates off to an early and strong start.

Networking meetings. It is also appropriate to arrange a weekly networking meeting for all candidates. These meetings are an ideal time not only for candidates to bring each other up to date on how their individual searches are progressing, but also a place where leads can be exchanged and mutual encouragement given. An ideal time for a networking meeting is Friday afternoon, another time when job interviews seldom occur and telephone calls to potential employers seldom get through. The session might even be called a "TGIF Session" and can provide an opportunity to let off steam and maintain energy for the next round of the job search or to celebrate someone's landing.

One-on-one counseling. Individual meetings between career consultants and their clients are held once a week or once every two weeks. The purpose is to review job strategy, resolve search issues such as lack of contacts, difficulty in writing cover letters, and so on, and motivate candidates for the next round of searching.

Job search manual. Each candidate should be issued a personal copy of a job search manual. The manual should contain directions for conducting various segments of the job search. In addition, it should contain blank forms that the candidate can fill in as the job search proceeds toward its conclusion. An ideal job search manual would contain sample cover letters and examples of résumés that a candidate might want to adapt. All outplacement firms have manuals that they provide to client firms, and some large organizations have their own to use in their internal transition centers.

Other Resources to Consider

Host visits by company recruiters. A career transition center is an ideal site to host a recruiter from a hiring company. The group meeting room can be used by the recruiter to give a detailed presentation about the company and its philosophy and culture and a description of the positions it is seeking to fill. The group presentation also allows an opportunity for questions from candidates. The recruiter can then either schedule interviews at the company site or conduct interviews with interested candidates in a private office at the career transition center.

Host visits by executive recruiters. Executive recruiters can visit the center to make presentations to candidates about the general nature of the local and regional job market. They can also give candidates tips on how to approach headhunters and inform them on the general procedures that are followed in sourcing, screening, interviewing, and selecting candidates. The recruiters will be motivated to conduct these visits because it will give them visibility among candidates who, when employed, are potential customers.

Host visits by venture capitalists. Venture capital firms are sometimes the source of employment leads for candidates who are senior managers or highly specialized individual contributors. Representatives of venture capital firms can conduct informational presentations on types of companies and products that they fund and, if appropriate, interview candidates with skills needed by these firms.

Résumé booklets. One project that the career transition center can engage in is the development of a booklet of candidate profiles or résumés. Copies of this booklet can be mailed to all local and regional firms that might be in a hiring mode. Career transition firms do this routinely—usually deleting the candidate's name and including only a short descriptive paragraph. Professional organizations frequently set up job placement areas and display notebooks of full résumés or available job positions. The booklet technique is very effective when the downsizing firm has a reputation for employing high quality workers—their loss can be another company's gain.

Invitation to other companies to recruit onsite. As with all onsite visits and recruiting, there are strong advantages to the host company, the recruiters, and the exiting employees. The goal is to help employees get placed successfully as quickly as possible. Again, one company's loss can be another's gain.

Job fairs. If a large downsizing is planned, the company might find it useful to host a job fair and invite companies whose business is similar or whose employees hold similar positions. It provides great public relations for the host company ("See how well they are treating their employees in this difficult situation.")

Determining Availability of Services

- What will be the hours of the service?
- How will shift personnel or those who work on weekends be handled?
- Will the services be available close to the original work site or close to transportation lines or residential areas?

Determining Duration of Services for Terminated Employees

AT&T provides career transition services for all terminated employees, both management and occupational, until they find a *permanent position*. The tricky part for career transition firms, centers, and corporations is defining *permanent position*. Does it include a long-term temporary assignment? What happens if the person takes the job and then quits after a month? What if a person works for a temporary agency? What about the individual who decides to become a consultant and then six months later decides to seek a full-time, permanent position?

Common variations in providing length of services include:

- Unlimited
- Twelve months
- Three, six, or nine months
- One-month "quick start" programs

Job searches typically take six to twelve months for managers and professionals. Job searching is a discouraging business that very few people enjoy or are successful at conducting. Job search services can quicken the time for job reentry.

Determining Who Receives the Services

Will all of the employees receive services or only the represented staff or managers at a certain level in the organization? The definition of the recipients needs to be clearly spelled out.

Setting Up an Internal Transfer System

An internal transfer system might include:

- An open job-posting system
- Policy requirements of giving internal transfers the first opportunity to apply for a position
- Finding incentives to encourage managers to hire, develop, and possibly retrain employees from one job classification into another

Open Job-posting System

An open job-posting system is a three-step process:

- It requires that all hiring managers write a job description for the position they want to fill, including a description of job functions and responsibilities and the skills, abilities, and experiences required of the successful applicant.
- It requires that the job be posted in such a manner that many people can see it and have the opportunity to apply.
- It encourages managers to interview more than one applicant who meets all of the requirements.

An open posting system works to everyone's benefit: the company's, the hiring manager's, and the prospective employee's. When a company clearly and openly states what positions are available, it tells everyone within the company and outside it about the kinds of employees it is looking for and the requirements for success. Many read between the lines and determine the quality level of the employees and the company, the kind of work that is being pursued, and the overall financial health and well-being of the organization. Through open posting, the company is also clearly stating to all of its employees and to the larger community that it not only believes in equal opportunity and is genuinely looking for the new employee with the best job fit, but also that it is taking action to ensure that it hires the best-qualified person.

An open posting system for the hiring manager is a mixed bag. Hiring managers are busy people and they don't want to be bothered with the time-consuming process of interviewing and selecting. They frequently argue that they have trained someone inside to take on the position or they know someone who can easily fill the job and be trained in it. An open posting system forces them to accurately describe the job function and requirements and to have that description subject to the scrutiny of others—their boss, their peers and competitors, and their subordinates. Managers who seek to maintain the vitality of an office find the open posting system to be a way to keep in touch with the quality level of job applicants and the range of experiences that a candidate can bring to the job.

For peers and "hopefuls," an open posting tells them what the job responsibilities and requirements are and encourages employee self-development efforts. If a person knows that a desirable job requires certain skills, they will seek to develop those skills and abilities. If employees know that they have a chance to increase their skill base, to be promoted, or to transfer into a lateral position, they generally are more strongly motivated to be productive for the organization. No one wants to feel stuck forever in a job. An open posting keeps employees motivated.

Admittedly, many jobs are claimed before they're posted or claimed without posting. In the long run, this is not healthy for the organization, which must face the onslaught of employee resentment, bitterness, and discouragement, conveyed by such remarks as, "There's not much point in working hard because it won't get you anywhere unless you know someone" or "It's not worth trying for the job because someone's probably already claimed it."

WHO GETS FIRST CRACK AT THE JOB POSTING? Some companies choose to only promote from within the system, others hire only externally, others are a mixture. The organizational culture and the goals and future direction of the company determine which course is better to take.

Some companies take pride in offering their employees a one- or two-week advance opportunity to apply for a position before the job is posted externally to the organization. Some offer jobs on an internal-posting-only basis when they have a hiring slowdown or freeze. Others ask their internal candidates to compete with external candidates on an equal basis: Both get the notices at the same time. Again, the company culture, goals, and directions determine the best policy.

WHO TAKES JOE?   One of the most challenging tasks for any company facing a downsizing is to figure out how to transfer people from one department to another, one profession to another, or one job classification to another. Internal negotiating, arm-twisting, and incentives are frequently required. An inplacement system works well for companies that want to keep employees who are now without a position because of downsizing, or want to transfer a competent employee who has a poor job fit, or simply want to encourage job rotation. Key staffing members get together and express their job needs and their employee transfer situations and then seek good job fits. The only limitations are the imagination and legal and ethical requirements. Major job shifts frequently mean retraining an employee (it doesn't matter at what level) and incorporating that employee into the work style of the new organization. The transfer pays off when the employee can bring a wide range of skills and abilities and, most importantly, a willingness to make the transfer. Orientation programs and clearly defined job responsibilities ease the transition. Career planning programs can help the employee define appropriate career transitions as well.

Checklist for Implementing an Internal Career Transition Center

❑ Geographic location
  • On current company site?
  • Located nearby?
  • Using rented space?
  • Located close to public transportation?
  • Close to potential employers?

❑ Physical facility
  • Size of facility (not too big, not too small)?

❑ Furnishings
  • Cubicles
  • Telephones
  • Computers
  • Copying machines
  • Fax machine
  • Supply cabinet
  • Candidate lockers or file drawers
  • Kitchen appliances
  • Air conditioning (central or window units)

- ❏ Office configuration
  - Training room(s)
  - Counselor office(s)
  - Receptionist area
  - Library area
  - Video room
  - Group meeting area
  - Bulletin board area
  - Candidate personal storage area
  - Coffee break room
- ❏ Career transition center management
  - Contract with Private Industry Council
  - Contract with outplacement/career transition firm
  - Contract with independent counselor
  - Contract with nonprofit organization
  - Use of internal resources
- ❏ Organizational function reported to
  - Human resources director
  - General manager
  - Chief financial officer
  - Other
- ❏ Staffing
  - Counselors
  - Librarian
  - Trainers
  - Receptionist
  - Word processor (for cover letters and résumé writing)
  - Manager
- ❏ Have available
  - Personal and crisis counselors (e.g., employee assistance personnel to handle possible psychological or substance abuse problems)
  - Benefits representatives
- ❏ Staffing options to consider
  - Use existing internal staff
  - Hire external adjunct counselors
  - Contract with outside organization
- ❏ Format of services to offer
  - Job search workshops
  - Networking or job club meetings
  - One-on-one counseling

❑ Other resources to consider
  • Find announcements bulletin boards?
  • Provide job search manuals?
  • Invite other companies to recruit on-site?
  • Host job fairs?
  • Host executive recruiters?
  • Host venture capitalists?
  • Computerized job databases or lists with mail-merge capability?

❑ Availability of services
  • Daily, 8 A.M. to 5 P.M.?
  • Mornings only?
  • Afternoons only?
  • Evenings?
  • Weekends?
  • Two or three days per week?

❑ Duration of services for terminated employees
  • Up to six months?
  • Less than one year?
  • Longer than one year?
  • As a permanent option?

❑ Who receives the services?
  • Executives and senior management?
  • Middle management?
  • Represented only?
  • All employees?
  • Spouses?

❑ Company culture
  • How does the center fit in with the existing organizational culture?
  • How might it reinforce an emerging culture?
  • What image should the career transition center portray?

❑ Cost
  • Is this a cost center (charged back to department budget)?
  • A break-even center?
  • A company-supported center?
  • A federally subsidized (JTPA) center?
  • How much will it cost to run an internal center? (Total cost? Cost per terminated employee?)

CAREER DEVELOPMENT AND
TRANSITION PROGRAMS IN COMPANIES

First Interstate Bank: A Full-Service Program

First Interstate Bank first developed its career services programs in 1983. The bank was going through a series of reorganizations and downsizings, and management was searching for a way to compassionately and quickly help those who were being laid off to find new positions—either within the bank or outside it. The newly created manager of career services developed a three-pronged focus to address management's and the employees' career concerns. Those three prongs, the transition center and outplacement services, the career development services group, and the internal job-posting function, have served a large number of people.

The transition center is primarily used by nonexempt staff. It's a regular career transition center with extensive job postings available from companies located in the nearby area. It provides counseling services to help people with stress, emotional, and substance abuse concerns; assistance with résumé writing and job interview skills; and a job search workshop, which they contract out to several vendors.

As with most companies, First Interstate contracts with outplacement firms to provide individualized services for their senior and executive officers. The mid- to senior-level managers are offered a four-month contract with a career transition firm. These firms also conduct a two-day onsite workshop program for midlevel officers and a one-day program for the hourly staff.

The career development services unit operates quite differently. The focus is on continuing career development throughout an employee's entire work history with the bank. The unit sponsors twenty-one workshops over the year, which are posted on a quarterly schedule. The unit sees itself as a positive function for people who are in transition (but not being laid off) in their careers, people who have questions about how to maintain their career vitality, and people who wonder if they're really in the right field. The manager of the career development services unit described the people who come into her center: "People come in to talk about their career direction. It's as if some have a rope with a knot at one end that they hold onto. They have no direction or aim. They just hold on and swing. We offer them career assessment and individualized career coaching. I just listen. They tell their story. They enter in black and white and leave in technicolor." That must be some powerful listening.

In 1991, the human resources department restructured and incorporated research and development functions into HR. The career planning services unit is part of the R & D orientation group.

For more information, contact the Manager of Career Resources, First Interstate Bank, Los Angeles.

Chemical Bank: An In-House Transition Center Using External Consultants

Another financial institution, Chemical Bank, also provides internal career counseling to all of their workforce. In 1991, they had 20,000 employees in the United States and 28,000 worldwide. David Rottman, the vice president of human resources and manager of career services, noted that banks everywhere are letting people go in large numbers primarily due to mergers, takeovers, and financial troubles. Those employees layed off from Chemical Bank who have the roughest time finding a new job are the ones who have to find a new profession, too. For example, the municipal bond traders are pretty much gone now. Those who only know dead or limited-use computer languages are struggling, as are those who had a generalized staff job and don't have a specialty.

The job search, however, is only part of the issue. Chemical Bank is a good place to work, and a lot of employees hired on with the idea that this would be their career home for all of their working lives. When they're laid off, they feel betrayed. They've been with the bank most of their career life, they like their jobs, they want to stay with Chemical Bank and, in fact, they expect to finish their careers with the Bank. They get very angry and upset when they're laid off. They feel a lot of grief over their loss of work and the "Bank family."

Chemical Bank relies heavily on external consultants for their internal career counseling services. Only 10 percent of the staff are Chemical Bank employees; the other 90 percent are adjunct counselors who are paid on an hourly basis. The criteria for being hired on a consulting basis are straightforward and demanding: demonstrated expertise in career counseling and good counseling skills. In addition, consultants must also be effective not only in one-on-one individual counseling but also in the stand-up delivery of workshop presentations. Sometimes they look for counselors who have expertise in some specialty areas such as data processing.

The in-house service is located in a building close to the headquarters building in New York City and has been available to people since 1983. According to Rottman, "It just grew organically and seems to have always been a part of the Bank. We catch people in a tough transition period. Only in retrospect are people grateful that we are here."

Career transition is offered to all terminating employees. Everyone gets three to five hours per week of one-on-one career counseling. There are "job search attack groups" of approximately six to seven people who meet once a week to develop strategy, reinforce the job search process, and keep each other motivated to keep knocking on employers' doors. The groups are heterogeneous so people have a chance to mix with a variety of professions. Every week there are lectures on a variety of topics, such as being an entrepreneur or networking.

The physical facilities are similar to a regular work environment: There are office carrels, a telephone answering service, word processing capabilities, and assistance with résumés and letters. This is a workplace and the task is to find a job. Everything that will help Chemical Bank employees make the transition smoothly and quickly is offered.

Terminating employees are assessed using one or more of a series of personality and interest inventories, generally the *Myers-Briggs Type Indicator®* (MBTI®) instrument, the *Strong Interest Inventory,®* the *16 PF,* and other similar instruments. Employees attend workshops where they identify their values, strengths, and interests. They develop an action plan for finding their next job, writing a résumé, and developing interviewing skills. The counselor's job is to work with their clients until they find a new job, even beyond the end of the four- to five-month severance period. Counselors are expected to switch back and forth between providing support one moment and, in the next, motivating people in their job search. About two-thirds of the effort goes toward training people in job search techniques and the other third toward giving morale boosts that will assist them in moving to the next phase of their careers and their lives. About one-third of their people find jobs in three to four months, another third find jobs in five to six months, and the last third take seven to twelve months. A very small number will take more than a year.

Chemical Bank sends a small number of people to external career transition firms. What do they look for in a firm? They look for a caring staff and a good match in ability and professional experience levels between the potential counselor and the client. The counselor needs to be a good strategic thinker. Rottman adds, "The firm is irrelevant. The counselor is more important. We meet the counselor first, see the location they're working in. Then we choose four or five firms and encourage our employees to shop a little." What is the impact of shopping? "It's good for the employee. It gives them the power of choice and the chance to grill the outplacement person. This is their career and their life and they can be a little choosy."

For more information, contact Vice President of Human Resources and Manager of Career Services, Chemical Bank, New York.

Pacific Bell: A Strong Internal Transition Program

Pacific Bell is that rare company that, up until the fall of 1991, offered their management virtually a lifetime job guarantee. If the employee performed well, there would be a job available. Yet they have been cutting back on their staff and actively downsizing since 1987. How do they do it?

Pacific Bell business heads pay close attention to their budget figures, to the work that is being performed, and to the people who are employed in their unit. When their funding is reduced, they are asked to assess the following:

- What work can be stopped?
- What work can be done better elsewhere?
- How can this work be done in a more cost-effective manner?
- What work and what positions are superfluous?

THE TRANSFER AND/OR OUTPLACEMENT PROCESS. At this point, human resources works with the business unit to relocate surplus employees. During the first sixty days that an employee searches for a job, HR looks for a lateral "commutable" position, that is, a job that is at the same level and is within commuting distance from where the employee currently lives. If no position has been found, then during the next sixty days, a search is made for a downgraded position that is within commuting distance or a lateral position that is out of commuting range and would require a move. Employees are carried until they receive at least one job offer. When they receive the offer, they have five business days to decide whether or not to accept it. Even if the new position is at a lower level and will require a relocation, it is considered an acceptable option. If they turn it down, then they are offered career transition services to find a position outside of Pacific Bell.

If an employee elects to leave, he or she gets 5 percent of his or her salary for each year of service for a maximum of one year severance pay. They also offer an early leave incentive of three months pay.

CAREER TRANSITION SERVICES.   Exiting supervisory and hourly staff are encouraged to participate in a two-day seminar and can receive ten hours of individual counseling and three hours of support services. They also have the option of getting Pacific Bell benefits for one year or paying their own COBRA coverage for eighteen months. Executives are placed with external outplacement firms that have a good reputation for being knowledgeable about the local area and can provide statewide services.

CODED OPEN JOB POSTINGS AND CODED EMPLOYEE PROFILES.   The job postings for management positions list all the requirements for the job and include a work experience code. Every individual receives a code and a worker profile that lists licenses, certificates, and relevant work experience. Then the matching begins. Those who are surplus employees get priority treatment over other non–Pacific Bell employees. It has taken considerable time to put together the codes for both the positions and for the employees' professional experiences. Now it is paying off very well for everyone. Currently, Pacific Bell is developing a database for all surplus employees to help them move more rapidly into a matching position.

As with most companies, Pacific Bell encourages employees to network within the company to find new positions. Not only is it easier for employees to relocate if they take the initiative to find out about and then apply for relevant positions themselves, but it's also one of the most important job skills that all jobholders are expected to develop.

For more information, contact Human Resources, Pacific Bell, San Ramon, CA.

Sun Microsystems: A Public-Private Partnership Model

In July 1991, Sun Microsystems, a Fortune 200 manufacturer of computer work stations, announced that it planned a restructuring that would result in the deployment, or layoff, of up to 900 nonexempt employees at their Milpitas, California, manufacturing facility. This announcement was quickly followed by the installation of a career resource and transition center at their Milpitas complex. The center is managed and staffed by the Career Action Center, a Palo Alto, California, "free standing" nonprofit career resource organization.

The center is staffed by four career management specialists from the Career Action Center and an employment specialist from Sun Microsystem's human resources department. The goal of the center is to provide career development resources for all Sun Microsystem employees and specifically to assist the deployed nonexempt employees to learn career planning and decision-making skills and to implement a successful job search, either inside or outside the company.

GROUP SEMINARS.   When employees learn that their jobs have been identified as "deployed," they attend a series of two- to three-hour seminars conducted by Career Action Center staff members. An orientation session, co-led by a Sun manager, acquaints employees with the scope of services available to them. In addition, the general labor market and economic trends that have precipitated their present situation are outlined and discussed. This presentation leads to the ventilation of employee feelings about their predicament. The orientation is followed by half-day workshops on self-assessment, job market research, résumé or job application forms, and interview skill training. The workshops, which are spread over a two-week time span, total twelve hours, and each is limited to fifteen individuals.

INDIVIDUAL COUNSELING.   In addition to the workshops, each employee receives four hours of individual consultation. This can be with a career counselor for assistance in career decision making or strategy planning, or it can be with the resource specialist to learn how to research and analyze job market information or to use the center's electronic databases.

OUTREACH ACTIVITIES.   In addition to the services provided by the transition center staff, there is a regular series of brown bag presentations by representatives from temporary employment agencies, job shops, local employers and job search experts.

THE TRANSITION CENTER'S PHYSICAL FACILITY.   The physical facility of the transition center includes the following:

Computer databases.   The center houses two electronic databases that generate national and state job listings. These are the National Employment Wire Service (NEWS) and Job Link.

Videos. Two videotape viewing stations are stocked with videotapes that showcase and explain various occupations and industries as well as skill-building tapes on résumés, interviewing, networking, and so forth. In addition, video recording and playback equipment is available for hands-on job interview practice and critique.

Bulletin boards. Several bulletin boards are placed throughout the transition center in easy-to-see high traffic areas. They contain simple job seeking hints as well as such practical items as a comprehensive list of job-hot-line telephone numbers and scheduled job fairs in the local area. An "It Works" bulletin board contains testimonials by job seekers who have succeeded in securing interviews and landing jobs. Another bulletin board features the weekly schedule of workshops, brown bag presentations, and special events. In addition, there are lists of professional and technical societies that employees might wish to establish contact with as well as listings of educational programs offered by the region's community colleges.

Employer files. The resource center includes a large bookcase of colorful three-ring binders that contain lists of employers, organized by type of industry. These binders contain profiles of each local company with information on size, product lines, and addresses and phone numbers of contact persons.

Job listings. Next to the employer files is an even larger bookcase of black three-ring binders that contain over 4,000 current job listings that have been sent by local employers to the Career Action Center. The job listings are updated daily and filed in the binders by type of industry. In addition to these outside job listings, there is a binder of current openings within Sun Microsystems that employees may apply for. An employment liaison specialist (an employee of Sun Microsystem's human resources department) is housed in the transition center to assist candidates in applying for internal openings.

Reference books. A bookcase next to the resource specialist's desk contains several shelves of reference books. These include the *Encyclopedia of Associations, Occupational Outlook Handbook, Dictionary of Occupational Titles,* and course catalogs for all of the local community colleges.

How-to books. In addition to the reference books, there are numerous how-to books such as *What Color is Your Parachute?* and several Fifty-Minute Books such as *Effective Networking* and *The Job Search That Works.*

Cubicles. The centers contains twenty-five individual office cubicles that candidates can use on a first-come–first-served basis. They need only sign up for a particular cubicle when arriving at the center. Each cubicle is equipped with a spacious desktop, a telephone, and a personal computer (some have IBM compatible PCs and others have Macintosh computers). The computers are networked into several laser and ink-jet printers located at strategic spots next to the cubicles. All computers are equipped with both word processing and résumé writing software. The telephones are programmed to access all five counties in the San Francisco Bay Area.

Office machines. A high-speed copy machine is located at the main entrance to the cubicle area and is available for use by all candidates. Two fax machines are also located in the cubicle area.

Computerized career system. The transition center is equipped with CareerPoint, a sophisticated computerized career planning system that features self-administered interest and personality style assessments as well as an action planning component.

Information about this public-private partnership career resource and transition center is available from Career Action Center, Palo Alto, CA.

Baxter Healthcare: An Internal Career Center Model

In 1986, Baxter Healthcare Corporation acquired American Hospital Supply. This merger resulted in significant duplication of staff members, prompting a downsizing. Baxter decided to establish an internal outplacement center, the Baxter Career Center, in Northbrook, Illinois, in a building a few miles from its corporate headquarters. The center is managed and staffed by a core group of two Baxter human resource managers and three Baxter clerical support/word processing specialists. Up to twenty independent consultants are hired on a part-time, as-needed basis to provide individual job search coaching and to lead career planning workshops.

Since 1986, the center has served the needs of a fluctuating group of from 200 to 900 outplaced employees each year. In addition, a small but steadily growing number of Baxter employees who are not affected by downsizing visit the center each year for assistance and/or support in career decision making.

GROUP SEMINARS.   When employees learn that their jobs have been eliminated, they attend a one-hour orientation session led by the career center manager. In this session, the manager acquaints the employees with the scope of services available to them. The orientation is followed by a two-day workshop on self-assessment, job market research, résumé or job application forms, and interview skill training. Each workshop participant receives a job search workbook and is encouraged to practice their telephone skills through role-play.

INDIVIDUAL COUNSELING.   Immediately following the workshop, each employee participates in an individual one-hour consultation with a career consultant to write a résumé. When approved by the consultant, the résumé is then given to the word processing center with a twenty-four-hour turnaround. Employees can then sign up with a counselor or job developer each week for job search coaching. There is no limit to the number of individual counseling appointments that a candidate can make.

JOB DEVELOPER.   A part-time consultant job developer is available by appointment to assist employees in contacting recruiters and in applying directly to companies. The job developer advises the employees on how to make networking calls to contacts at external companies.

THE TRANSITION CENTER'S PHYSICAL FACILITY.   The physical facility of the transition center includes the following:

Videos.   Video recording and playback equipment is available for hands-on job interview practice and critique. Interview practice sessions can be scheduled with a consultant.

Resource room.   The resource room contains several shelves of reference books as well as local and out-of-town newspapers. Reference books include the *Encyclopedia of Associations, Occupational Outlook Handbook, Dictionary of Occupational Titles,* and entrepreneurial materials for employees interested in pursuing self-employment opportunities. None of the books and periodicals may be removed from the resource room, but a copy machine is readily available, and employees are encouraged to copy items for use in their job search.

External job bank.   The center's resource room includes a bank of companies and recruiters who have provided job orders directly to the career center. Three-ring binders contain summaries of open positions as well as detailed information on each job. Jobs are categorized both alphabetically and functionally. A bulletin board displays the most current openings. A historical list of all companies and jobs that have been listed since the establishment of the center contains valuable networking contact persons at each company.

Internal job bank. A second job bank contains current openings within Baxter Healthcare Corporation that employees may apply for. Employees have until thirty days after their termination date to self-nominate for up to two internal jobs as a current employee. After thirty days, they must compete with nonemployees. The internal job bank contains descriptions of open jobs, requisition numbers, and salary information. As in the external bank, recently opened internal jobs are posted on a bulletin board.

Job club. Job club sessions are led periodically by a consultant. They include discussions and practice on a variety of job search techniques and are designed to build both skill and motivation.

Cubicles. The center contains forty-four individual office cubicles and a half-dozen private offices that candidates can use on a first-come–first-served basis. They need only tell the receptionist which particular cubicle they will be using in the center. Each cubicle is equipped with a spacious desktop and a telephone. The telephones are programmed to access any area of the country where jobs are likely be found. There are typewriters available in some cubicles. In past months, when the number of displaced workers was higher, the center expanded to quarters on the next floor where they added 200-plus cubicles.

Office machines center. A copy machine, word processing equipment (Lotus and LaserJet printer) and a fax machine are located near the cubicle area. The office machine center is operated by two full-time word processing specialists.

Information about this model internal career center is available from Manager, Career Continuation Center, or Manager of Career Transition Services, at Baxter Healthcare Corporation, Northbrook, IL.

THE BRIDGE
TO THE FUTURE

10

Getting On With Business

Randy Larson, a specialist in Streeter-Haaz's research division, had been the first one in the office the morning after the layoffs. It was only 7:30 A.M. and work generally didn't start until a little past 8:00. Getting to work that early had been a little unusual for Randy. Normally he commuted in a carpool with his supervisor, John Torres, and with an administrative assistant in the human resources department, Alice McKinsey. But all that had changed.

Both John and Alice had been laid off the day before. They were part of the 176-person reduction in force. Since it had been his week to drive, Randy drove all three of them to work that morning. None of them had any idea that the rumored layoff would hit so close to home. John had told him about his layoff as they were getting ready for their morning break: John wouldn't need a ride home; his wife would drive in and pick him up. Alice had called Randy at 11:00 A.M. to tell him that she, too, was laid off and would not need a ride home.

Even though twenty-four hours had passed, Randy had still felt shocked and confused. John's son, Jack, and his son, Nicholas, played on the same Little League team. What would he say to John when he saw him at the Saturday game? he wondered. And what about Alice, who was a single mother and had been really struggling to make ends meet when she had landed her job last year. Randy had felt utterly helpless and hopeless. He had no idea what he would say or do should he run into either John or Alice.

And what about the research group? They had lost seven people, including their supervisor, John. Everyone now reported directly to Sara Piatt, the advanced systems research group manager and vice president of research. Randy had liked Sara, even though he had only had superficial contact with her in the past. John had hired and trained him. John had been a good supervisor and a good friend, too.

What would happen in the group? Would the twelve people who were left be expected to assume the workload of nineteen?

Then Randy had noticed a memo on his desk. Sara must have put it there after he had left the night before. The memo said that Sara had scheduled a survivors meeting for the remaining twelve members of the group for 10:30 that morning. The meeting would run until 1:30 in the afternoon, and lunch would be brought in.

A survivors meeting. Randy wondered what that meant.

SURVIVOR TRAINING

With the phenomenal growth of the outplacement field during the past decade, almost all of the technical development and changes have been limited to two areas: (a) preplanning assistance for corporate management and (b) services to the outplaced candidate. Very little has been done for the survivors of downsizing until recently. The survivors are an extremely important element in the downsizing scenario. Earlier, we commented on how analogous being fired or laid off is to the death of a loved one. Our society has developed elaborate and useful rituals to deal with the death of a loved one. We have wakes and funerals. Family and friends come to the home of the survivors after the funeral with food to nurture the survivors. These rituals are not for the dead. They are designed to assist the survivors in coping with the grief of the loss, to help them say good-bye to the departed, and to help them focus on how to move forward with their lives.

As a society, we have not yet institutionalized rituals for dealing effectively with the loss of a job or career. In business, we have many rituals that are analogous to family celebrations. Companies have ceremonies to "christen" a new building or a new product line. They have parties to celebrate the company birthday. Company rites of passage such as individual promotions and growing beyond income or sales benchmarks are celebrated. But until very recently, very little has been done to assist the survivors of a downsizing, to acknowledge the loss of team members and then move forward. Some have said that the most important players in the downsizing scenario are the survivors. After all, they are the ones who will be responsible for preventing a reoccurrence of the business problems that necessitated the current downsizing. If the survivors, who are the ongoing strategic workforce, are paralyzed with feelings of loss and helplessness, how can they move the company forward? If they feel guilt over the loss of a colleague while they are still on the payroll, how can they express the positive attitude and morale that will be necessary to turn a profit next quarter? Survivor training is an effective way to acknowledge the corporate changes and to move from being a survivor to being a part of the strategic workforce.

It is useful to set up a meeting with the survivors within seventy-two hours of a group termination if possible. There are several options for who conducts the meeting: an internal or external organizational development specialist, an outplacement consultant, or someone who is external to the downsized group. In other words, it should be conducted by someone who can be an objective facilitator. The participants of the survival workshop are the immediate group of peers and subordinates that worked on a daily basis with the terminated employee(s), the department, the office, or the management team.

A Practical Training Model

An effective survivor training model, outlined in figure 10, involves a three-hour session with a catered lunch. No more than twenty-five to thirty persons should be involved in this group. The training can be conducted on-site in a department conference room or off-site at a local hotel.

Sara Piatt, the vice president of research, entered the room and conversed with a few of the early arrivals. She was tired and worried. After all, her department had lost several good researchers, technicians, and clerical staff. Not only that, one of her most promising projects had been canceled. Streeter-Haaz had decided to go with proven results. She had

Number of participants		25 to 40
Length of session		3 hours
Purpose		• To surface and deal with concerns about the fate of the terminated employees and the future of the survivors
		• To move from reactive survivors to proactive members of the strategic workforce
Presenters		CEO, department manager, and transition management consultant (internal or external)
Time	*Who*	*Topic and description*
10 min.	CEO	Introduction: Rationale for downsizing
20 min.	Consultant	Discussion: Venting of feelings
20 min.	Consultant	Short lecture: Transitional stages
20 min.	Consultant	Discussion: How to help terminated colleagues
60 min.	Consultant	Informal group lunch
50 min.	Consultant & Department Manager	Discussion: How to best get on with the work of the department without the help of the terminated colleagues

Figure 10   Sample Agenda for Survivor Training Session

stayed up late at night trying to figure out what direction to take and how to manage with a reduced workforce. Now she needed to inspire the staff that remained. They called themselves the survivors, a bittersweet term. She knew that they needed to see themselves as the strategic workforce—a workforce that did more than survive, one that moved the department and the company forward. It was 10:30 A.M. and Streeter-Haaz president Stuart Aubret entered the room to begin the session.

During the first ten minutes, Stuart sketched out the business and economic scenario that led to the downsizing. "We reduced capital expenditures by 63 percent, and I instituted a number of cost-cutting measures, including restrictions on travel and hiring. In addition, all senior managers, senior vice presidents, and I volunteered to take a 5 to 7 percent salary reduction. Unfortunately, that was not enough. The management team and I had to make the painful decision to close down the SK line. Based on budget projections for this next year, we do not anticipate any more layoffs. *[Note: This important message is stated only if, to the president's knowledge, it is true.]* If you have questions about the downsizing, please ask. I look to each of you to help me, the research department, and Streeter-Haaz to rethink and retool our operation so that we can emerge a strong and powerful unit this next year and in the future. You are the strategic workforce that will make the future happen. I look forward to working with you in this new phase. At this point, I will turn the meeting over to your department manager, Sara Piatt, and to Ray Morse, our transition consultant, who is working with several managers at Streeter-Haaz."

The survivor session should begin with a brief ten-minute presentation. The president should give the big picture by sketching out the business and economic scenario that led up to the downsizing. This should include brief comments on other solutions that were considered and the rationale for selecting termination. If there were no additional layoffs planned, the manager should state that this is the only planned termination. Once again, this should be stated only if, to the department manager's knowledge, it is true. If appropriate, the manager can comment on why the specific positions were eliminated. This presentation should be followed by five to ten minutes of the president fielding questions about the decision to downsize. Once all questions have been answered, the president can leave the meeting.

Once the president has left, the consultant might comment on the president's presentation as being logical and businesslike and having presented the big picture clearly and rationally, but state that now is the time to discuss the human impact and the emotional ramifications. After all, the people laid off were more then colleagues; in many cases they were friends of the survivors. The consultant then walks to a flip chart and easel at the front of the room and asks, "How are you feeling right now? How did you feel when you got the word your colleagues were laid off?" If nobody volunteers, the consultant may need to probe. One technique is to go around the room clockwise and ask each person how he or she felt upon first hearing the news. This is effective in getting all of the survivors to verbalize their feelings. Some common feelings that are volunteered include:

- "I felt guilty because it wasn't me."
- "I felt the department was betrayed by the company."
- "I was shocked, and I didn't know what to say to Bob (or Sam or Alice)."
- "I was embarrassed. I still am. I don't know what to say when I see her in town."
- "I feel relieved. I felt something was going to happen. I'm glad it's over."

- "I feel really uneasy. I don't know when the ax will fall again. Maybe it will be me that gets laid off next."
- "I used to feel in control of my destiny. Now I don't know."

After the group's feelings have been verbalized and written on sheets of flipchart paper, they are taped to the wall in front of the room. The consultant then gives a short presentation/discussion about the emotional responses that the group has expressed, including the following points:

- Experiencing an emotional reaction to the termination of a friend or colleague is normal and expected. Not having any strong feelings would be unnatural. Not dealing with and expressing these feelings would be unhealthy. Talking about feelings in this group is healthy.
- There are three major life traumas. They are (a) the death of a loved one, (b) divorce or termination of a long-term relationship, and (c) the loss of a job. For most people, a major component of personal identity is the job. So, when the job is taken away, some of their personal identity goes, too.
- A model developed by Elizabeth Kubler-Ross can be helpful in understanding emotional responses to these three life crises. A rough approximation of Kubler-Ross' model suggests that we all go through a predictable roller coaster of emotions. These emotions are shock, disbelief, anger, bargaining, frustration, grief, and, finally, resolution.

The consultant can then move from the theoretical model to the very practical subject of just what is happening to their terminated colleagues and what the group can do to assist them in the transition.

What specific help is the terminated colleague getting now? The consultant describes the career transition services that their colleague is receiving. The consultant should stress that career transition includes assistance with dealing with the emotional roller coaster that the colleague is experiencing. While it is probably more intense and severe than the emotions that the survivors are experiencing, the emotions are probably progressing in a similar order to those of the survivors. The practical job search assistance such as office support, message service, video supported interview practice, résumé preparation, and salary negotiation training is described and discussed.

How can a colleague help the terminated employee? The terminated colleague can use more assistance than he or she is receiving from the career transition services. The survivors need to be reassured that they don't have to have a solid lead for a job in order to assist their colleague. What they should offer is whatever assistance they can give. For instance, any colleague can offer to read and critique a person's résumé. Everyone can think of some local organization that may need the skills this colleague has. And everyone has friends and acquaintances whom colleagues can be referred to. The referral doesn't have to have a solid job, but it may lead somewhere else. The most important point is to straightforwardly offer support and assistance. By working through ambivalent feelings about the termination, the survivors will feel more comfortable talking with their terminated colleagues. Without working through those feelings, the survivors often don't know what to say and will avoid social contacts because of embarrassment.

GETTING ON WITH THE WORK
OF THE DEPARTMENT

In addition to helping the terminated employees, how do the survivors get on with the work of the department? When a department has lost one or more important employees, the survivors must pull together to get on with their lives.

To continue the survivor training session described in this chapter, after the discussion on helping terminated employees has come to a close, an informal working lunch is served during which the consultant leads a discussion on how the survivors can pull together to get on with the work of the organization (or department, or project, etc.). The department manager plays a dual role. On one hand, he or she is just a member of the group that has to get on with the business of work. On the other hand, the manager possesses special knowledge and skills that the group will need to call on.

In a brainstorming session, the survivors are asked to list all of the work tasks that the department was involved in prior to the downsizing. In addition, they are asked to list any new or additional work tasks that the department might have to take on in the next few months. All of these tasks are written on a board or flip chart at the front of the room, and the group is asked to divide the work tasks into three groups:

- Absolutely necessary for the survival of the department/company

- Important, but not necessarily critical for survival

- Good to do, but the department/company can do well without it

Sometimes a fourth category, "Not necessary at all," naturally emerges at this point. If so, it should be included in the process.

The names of each of the surviving employees (who are now being called "the strategic workforce") are entered across the top of a matrix. Each of the "Absolutely necessary" work tasks are entered down the vertical axis of the matrix. Using consensus, the group puts an X in each cell of the matrix that represents a good match between an employee's *ability* and a particular work task.

The group facilitator then polls each member of the group about his or her motivation to perform each of the critical work tasks and enters a circle in each cell that represents a good match between an employee's *motivation* and a particular work task.

Resulting matrices are presented in tables 6 and 7.

The same process is repeated on the "Important, but not critical" and the "Good to do" categories.

The group is then asked to spend some time during the next week to consider the competency and motivation loading of the group, meeting for a half day to hammer out a proposal on how the department tasks might best be allocated among the department members. They are asked to consider the following points:

- Matching persons with high competency to critical tasks

- Matching persons to tasks where they express high motivation

- Delegating critical and important tasks to current staff

- Ensuring equitable and fair distribution of work among the staff

Table 6 Employee Abilities and Critical Work Tasks

	Strategic Workforce							
	Alice	John	Sam	Tran	Geo	Mark	Liza	Juan
Critical Work Tasks								
Compiling statistics	X		X	X	X	X	X	X
Analyzing sales activity	X		X		X	X	X	
Developing budgets		X	X			X	X	
Visiting field sites	X	X			X	X	X	X
Typing reports	X	X	X	X	X	X	X	X
Training field staff							X	X
Answering phones	X	X	X	X	X	X	X	X
Conducting research	X		X		X	X	X	X

Table 7 Employee Abilities and Critical Work Tasks

	Strategic Workforce							
	Alice	John	Sam	Tran	Geo	Mark	Liza	Juan
Critical Work Tasks								
Compiling statistics	O	O		O	O	O		
Analyzing sales activity		O	O	O		O		O
Developing budgets			O	O				
Visiting field sites		O		O			O	O
Typing reports	O		O					
Training field staff							O	O
Answering phones	O		O			O		O
Conducting research		O	O	O	O	O	O	

The department manager evaluates the feasibility of the new structure and meets with the strategic workforce staff to implement those aspects of the plan that prove feasible. The manager has had the opportunity (and responsibility) during the group sessions to give periodic feedback on the reality of many of the suggestions.

This process, when led by a competent facilitator and with the authentic cooperation of senior management, can contribute significantly toward a swift and productive recovery from the trauma of a downsizing. While it is natural and appropriate to look first inside the organization, to the survivors, it is also important to deal promptly with the external world.

ANNOUNCING THE DOWNSIZING TO THE OUTSIDE WORLD

Nathan Gottleib, Streeter-Haaz's director of communications, had just left a meeting with the president and his immediate staff. The topic of the meeting had been the decision to cut staff. As Nathan walked through the plush lobby and past Sam, the security guard, his mind flashed back to a television news program that he had seen eight years earlier.

Downsizing was a subject that Nathan was familiar with. Eight years ago he had been a reporter for the business section of the major newspaper in North Carolina's Tri-City. Much of his reporting had been on the apparently unending growth of the young high-tech firms—it was not uncommon for one of these young firms to double their personnel strength every year or so.

Nathan thought about the six o'clock news show that had opened his eyes to downsizing. Sally Wu, the news anchor, had announced that Xanadu, a high profile software manufacturer, had laid off 200 employees that morning. She indicated that she would have an interview with one of the laid-off workers on the eleven o'clock news. Later that night, Nathan caught the interview with Brian Williams, a software designer who had been laid off that morning. His description was vivid. When they had arrived at work that morning, Brian and all the people in his work group were told to report to the auditorium for a special company meeting. Once in the office, Brian noticed two uniformed security guards posted by each of the auditorium's four doors. The human resources manager took the podium and announced that declining sales had required that Xanadu take drastic steps to reduce losses. All of their jobs had been eliminated, effective that morning. They were not to go back to their offices. Their personal belongings were being boxed up and would be available for pick-up at the security shack in the parking lot that afternoon. They were told to form two lines before security guards, who took their company keys, photo I.D. badges, and company credit cards. Another guard checked their names off a list and handed them their final paychecks. The guards then escorted them to the parking lot. Brian felt stunned. He said he felt like a "lamb being led to slaughter."

Nathan Gottlieb shuddered as he remembered that news broadcast and the outpouring of anger that was directed toward Xanadu Corporation during the subsequent months. He vowed to do everything he could to keep Streeter-Haaz from duplicating Xanadu's errors.

The CEO is a key player in announcing the downsizing. In a case such as Xanadu's, the CEO is a much more appropriate choice to announce the downsizing to the affected employees than the human resources manager. It is appropriate for the CEO to comment on many of the alternatives to downsizing that were tried and to emphasize that this move was the last resort. The CEO should also issue a news release that outlines the downsizing and, if appropriate, appear on radio or television to discuss the downsizing and describe what is being done for the affected employees.

(It is interesting to note that following the summer announcement of the Bank of America/Security Pacific merger, a "leaked" Security Pacific memo revealed very favorable severance benefits, which shifted much of the press speculation from how many employees might be laid off to focusing on how well the company was treating the employees it was losing.)

Timing is an important factor in the announcement of a downsizing. If employees are to be notified on Tuesday morning at 9:00 A.M. that their jobs will be (or have been) eliminated, it is a good idea to have a news release detailing the particulars of the downsizing simultaneously hand-delivered to all local news media—daily newspapers, business journals, radio stations, television stations, and so on. That evening, the CEO might be interviewed on the six o'clock news. The human resources manager might be interviewed on the eleven o'clock news. The focus is on what is being done to assist the rank-and-file employees in terms of severance pay and reemployment assistance. Figure 11 presents a sample news release that gives the facts in a favorable light to the public.

Rumors fly fast. The company cannot keep the public, its customers and suppliers, and the business community from hearing about a downsizing. What the company can do is control what the public hears and how quickly it hears it. All written announcements pertaining to the downsizing should be carefully written. And they should be written as though they might be leaked and read on the six o'clock news. In chapter 6, we included copies of memos to employees that referred to corporate health, notification of termination, benefits calculation, severance pay, and retirement planning. Great care should be exercised in drafting these letters. Even though they are internal memos, there is a very good chance that they will fall into the hands of someone outside the organization—maybe even a reporter for the local business newspaper. A good rule of thumb when preparing such memos is to write them as if you expect it to be published on the front page of the *New York Times*.

SUMMARY

The survivors, the company's strategic workforce, need attention immediately following a restructuring. They need to know from their senior managers and their immediate managers what has happened and why. A meeting that supports venting and getting on with business reduces the time survivors spend feeling guilty and worried about what has happened to their colleagues, what they should say to them, and what is going to happen next. The strategic workforce meeting can be shifted into a planning session with the major tasks outlined and the work reconfigured based on skills and interests. It is important to have the ongoing workforce involved in the planning.

While the strategic workforce is meeting, public relations efforts must be immediate and ongoing. Press releases to the media need to be prepared in advance and delivered at the time of the announcement to the employees; senior management should be prepared to make a public statement outlining the strategies used to eliminate the problems and the reason for the restructuring now. They also need to tell the world about the services being provided for the terminated employees. Companies always need customers, and good public relations can help retain them.

STREETER-HAAZ CORPORATION

For Immediate Release

May 19, 1994
Contact: Nathan Gottleib at (601) 555-1313

Streeter-Haaz, a local manufacturer of information processing equipment, announced today that it was laying off 176 employees at its Green Street facility. The 176 employees represent 10 percent of Streeter-Haaz's workforce. Streeter-Haaz CEO Stuart Aubret indicated that the reduction in force was necessitated by the decline in orders for its SK-2000 and, to a lesser extent, the related MK series of products.

Last month Streeter-Haaz instituted a number of cost-cutting procedures, including reduced capital expenditures, curtailment of noncritical travel, postponement of off-site training, and a hiring freeze. All senior executives also took 5 to 7 percent pay cuts.

Streeter-Haaz's human resources vice president, Christina Perugia, indicated that all 176 employees were being offered extensive job search assistance as well as severance pay.

Figure 11   Sample News Release

Checklist for Getting On With Business

❏ The Strategic Workforce
  - Set up meeting places
  - Arrange for lunch
  - Prepare for meeting with consultant
❏ Public Relations
  - Identify one person to respond to the media (e.g., public relations manager)
  - Prepare public statements in advance of the downsizing
    - Rationale for restructuring
    - Other tactics tried
    - How many people are affected
    - What is being done for them
  - Distribute written copy to newspapers, radio, television
  - Prepare the CEO and human resources manager for their televised/video statements (which can also be used in communiques to employees)

11

The Strategic Workforce

Bob Wong, Streeter-Haaz's manager of finance and accounting, leaned back wearily in his chair. It was 10:00 P.M. and he was home looking at twenty-five pieces of paper—each one a note with a different person's name on it. The slips of paper represented his reconfigured organization—how it looked after the downsizing.

He remembered the last time he had had to deal with a downsizing and how stressful it had been. He would never forget having had to tell Lola Fernandez, his accounts payable manager and a valuable employee he had mentored, that because of the restructuring her job had been eliminated. Her expression had been devastating. Not only had he felt badly for her, he felt badly for himself. Lola had been with the company for twenty-two years and had developed strong, productive relationships with the accounts receivable department, the payroll group, the budget office, and vendors. She knew the history of the processes and could resolve difficult situations before they became problems. He had also had to lay off five of her staff, leaving just nine of them to do the work of fourteen people.

Bob hadn't known about the restructuring himself until the day before it had happened. He had had to tell the rest of the office staff what had happened and somehow get them productive again. The word had gone around the office in a flash that morning. Some of the group had just huddled down at their desks and kept quiet, while others had gotten on the phone to tell the rest of the organization. One thing was for sure: No one did any productive work that day—or for many days thereafter. Productivity and morale were low for weeks, maybe even months.

But that night, as Bob moved the little pieces of paper around into the new organizational structure, he knew that the next day would be much different than that day two years earlier.

This time, the managers had received training on how to conduct humane terminations, career transition services for the affected employees were already in place, and survivor training and organizational redesign meetings had already been conducted. Furthermore, the career development program that Streeter-Haaz instituted last spring had had the positive effect of empowering many of the employees to take charge of their careers and jobs. The whole concept of work had been rethought by Streeter-Haaz during the past eighteen months: Functions had been consolidated; new technology had been introduced; several layers of management had been removed to produce a more flexible workforce; and decision making had been pushed down to the individuals "in the trenches."

Two years earlier, Bob would have been overwhelmed by what was ahead. But that night, looking at his scraps of paper, he had a sense that this time things would be very different.

During a restructuring, the needs of employees whose jobs are being eliminated take center stage. But these people are not the only ones affected. Restructuring also creates a profound impact on the organization's ongoing employees—the strategic workforce.

REACTIONS OF THE SURVIVORS

Those not selected for termination presumably have the talent and background essential for carrying the organization forward in its new direction. Many will have the core knowledge, connections, experience, and sense of corporate history that will ease the transition from the old ways to the new ways. The organization will count on these survivors to unleash its potential.

However, they are not quite the same people they were before the downsizing. In fact, they share many of the turbulent emotions felt by those who were laid off. Their friends, colleagues, even supervisors may be telling them that they are lucky to hold on to their jobs, but they do not feel lucky. They miss their former group, their old leadership, and their friends in other departments. Although many of them look forward to new ways of doing business and even to new bosses and new opportunities, they were trained and rewarded for achieving the old corporate mission, and now they lack a clear sense of direction. They are burdened not only with extra work but also with fear and uncertainty and may be asking themselves many questions.

The "missed bullet" syndrome. Why wasn't I laid off? It could have been me. Actually, I'm not as skilled as Larry and he got laid off. And Arlene has been here longer than I. Why them and not me?

Work duties and hours. How will the work be redistributed? Will I be expected to work longer hours for the same pay? Will I be fired if I don't? Will some of the functions disappear? Will my job be the next to go? Are my skills needed? If so, how and for how long?

Performance expectations. What are the organizational priorities now? What am I supposed to do? What levels of quality and quantity are expected? Do I have what it takes to succeed—whatever that is?

Training and learning on the job. How will I learn the new tasks? How long will it take? Will I be vulnerable for the next downsizing if I don't learn right away? Who will teach me? Who will answer my questions?

Who's in charge? Do the new supervisors know what they are doing? What is the organizational structure? Has my unit lost or gained status? Am I being disloyal to my old boss if I help the new one succeed?

Loyalty. Can I be loyal to the newly restructured company? Or, since it fired all my friends, is it undeserving of respect? Should I just forget about respect, take care of myself, and screw the company?

Underlying all these work-related questions are strong and jumbled emotions. Employees will feel:

- Angry at the company and its management
- Suspicious of management's announcements
- Insecure, defensive, and turf-protective
- Relieved that this wave of layoffs is over
- Guilty that they remain while others were fired
- Indecisive and fearful of taking risks
- Saddened by the loss of their colleagues
- Bitter and disillusioned regarding organizational claims of "teamwork" and "workplace community"

These emotional effects will be less damaging if the organization has taken care to prune rationally and has accompanied the process with broad, effective, and honest communications. If people feel that the layoff was fair and understandable and that they were not deceived, they will be less hostile. But the pain will still exist. The CEO, senior and middle managers, and especially the first-line supervisors need to address the feelings of their workforce both directly, through one-on-one or group meetings, and indirectly, through paying attention to work assignments and ensuring a work environment that satisfies motivational needs.

Managing feelings, their own or anyone else's, is not something managers are trained to do. They are often surprised and nonplussed by the snide comments, the sudden tears, the displays of short temper, the "who cares?" shrugs on the part of formerly rational, enthusiastic employees. Although they often feel the same emotions that plague their staffs (after all, they are employees, too), they believe they are supposed to deny these emotions to set a good example. Add to this the additional burden of being the bearer of bad news and of having to figure out some way to pick up and rearrange the pieces, and it is not suprising that they are vulnerable to the paralysis that seeps through an organization during a downsizing. They would prefer to close their doors and bury themselves in work.

However, a downsizing calls for just the opposite behavior. In order to move the survivors out of "survivor mode" and into "constructive mode" as soon as possible, managers need to increase, not decrease, their accessibility and their active communications. Lost and confused, employees who have survived a layoff yearn for a sense of direction and, though they look somewhat numb, are actually eager to move forward. They require plenty of information—about where the organization is going, not where it came from—and they also need to be heard.

Tandem Computers, which was forced by industry slowdowns and market reversals to lay off six percent of its workforce, managed to retain some employee loyalty and productivity by communicating extensively and by encouraging employees to speak up about their feelings. Through the restructuring, the company maintained its open-door policy as well as an electronic-mail channel through which any employee can anonymously question a top executive.

RETHINKING THE CONCEPT OF WORK

It is unrealistic to expect the remaining employees, most of whom have not even regained their full energy and commitment, to continue to do all their own work in addition to that of the people who were laid off. However, the organization should not be allowed to bloat up again like a yo-yo dieter who resumes excessive eating. The following questions may provide some structure for rethinking the workload.

What work no longer has to be done?   If the downsizing were part of a rational plan to begin with, and not simply a slash-and-burn exercise, nonessential tasks have already been identified. What tasks *related* to these can also be eliminated? Which ones have little or nothing to do with the organization's new strategy? What unnecessary work can be taken out of jobs?

What functions can be consolidated?   The downsizing has undoubtedly resulted in fewer middle managers. Can some of their units be combined and redundant functions eliminated? Can training classes be combined?

How can processes be streamlined?   Can a product or service be delivered to the customer *in a way that satisfies the customer's requirements* more efficiently by eliminating certain steps?

How can we make better use of technology?   Existing hardware can be used in thousands of new ways to simplify work: to replace slow, hand methods, to increase collaborative synergy, to train employees, and to speed group decision making. Sometimes it is not even necessary to purchase new software; old software can be adapted.

What can we do differently to improve competitiveness without adding extra work? Can we redesign tasks and processes to create new types of service for our customers?

Such questions lead to a more basic one: Is the old concept of a *job* obsolete? A *job,* as organizations have been trained to think of it, is a set of static, predetermined duties. People are hired or promoted according to how well they fit certain job descriptions that tend to be one-shot assessments of what is needed at a particular point in time. These descriptions become frozen in place while technological advances and competitive challenges roar past. But without job descriptions, how would people know what their responsibilities are?

To unlock potential and respond to changing marketplace dynamics, it is more productive to think in terms of *roles* rather than jobs. Jobs may be eliminated, but workers can fulfill similar roles in new functions. As they practice and hone certain skills—specific technical skills or generic managerial skills such as problem analysis, decision making, and communication—they can qualify for increased responsibility and compensation, even if there is no job box that exactly matches their performance level and skill type. The *fluid roles* concept allows work to be revised and people to grow according to their individual strengths, even in a dynamically resizing organization. Roles can be linked to steps in the career ladder, much as jobs can. But because roles are described by skills and competencies rather than by units and functions, they are more flexible. Loss of a particular position because of job obsolescence need not necessarily mean loss of a skilled and competent employee who can play an identical or similar role elsewhere in the organization.

When downsizing eliminates layers of middle management, employees become responsible for their own work and the old command-and-control mentality begins to dissolve. Employees become, in many ways, self-supervising. This is appropriate, since organizations are moving away from paternalism and are no longer in a position to promise career security.

Some employees are developing a self-reliance based upon their work skills, their ability to maintain a job-related network of contacts, and their well-developed selling skills. Others are not accustomed to being in charge of new tasks or of their own career development, and they may need encouragement through training programs and internal communications efforts.

One company, British Petroleum, provided such encouragement in the form of a personal development planning program that employees could use to improve their skills, their performance, and their job satisfaction, as well as to make themselves more marketable. Although much of the program involved self-directed exercises with the use of a guidebook, it also required the active participation of the employee's supervisor. Together, supervisor and employee sought answers to such questions as, How can this be done? If interests and values do not mesh with the current position, what other positions are available inside or outside the job descriptions? Moving to another organization no longer carries the stigma it once did, so managers can and should discuss the possibility openly with their employees.

STAYING FLEXIBLE

In order to minimize the disruptions associated with downsizing and prevent "rebloating," employers have been rethinking workforce structure as well as the nature of work itself. No longer do they feel the need to "own" workers. Increasingly, they are relying on a flexible contingent workforce composed of part-timers, temporaries, and independent contractors. A study by Cornell University predicted that by that watershed year 2000, 43 percent of the support staff and 7 percent of managers in service companies will be contingent workers.

Companies have developed various ways of integrating the flexible workforce into the core group. Some temporaries, who include engineers, executives, accountants, and "rent a techs," as well as clericals, are hired by employment agencies, while others are given short-term assignments on the payroll of the core organization. Companies allocate spaces for consultants, and employees spend time working in the consultants' headquarters. Both part-time and full-time staff may include telecommuters who work primarily at home. Some contingent workers are former full-time employees.

When downsizing becomes necessary, it is usually simpler and less disruptive to focus first on the contingent workers, whose jobs have always been dependent on the fluctuating needs of the organization. However, a peripheral workforce does present certain management challenges, from determining benefits to the psychological risks of creating second-class workers. Organizations need to stay flexible enough to bring contingent workers into the full-time core workforce and help core people change their status to contingency, as skill requirements evolve. Core status should be based not on seniority but on contribution to the future of the core business.

THE FUTURE WORKFORCE

During and after a downsizing, management needs to be thinking not only about incumbents who have survived the layoffs but also about the other part of the strategic workforce: new hires (permanent or temporary, part-time or full-time) who will join these incumbents in propelling the organization toward its new goals. What choices does the organization have, and how can it attract the employees it most desires so that further resizing can be minimized?

By now, *Workforce 2000,* the 1987 Hudson Institute study commissioned for the Department of Labor, is well known. Those who are entering the workplace are older, have changed jobs more often, and probably have dependent care responsibilities. This entering workforce, which includes managers as well as nonmanagers, is multicultural, multilingual, and multiracial, and each group brings with it different value systems, behaviors, and goals. For organizations that are expanding globally (and their numbers are increasing), these cultural differences are magnified.

Why should organizations care about employees' values and goals? There are two reasons: The competition for highly skilled workers is increasing; and the employees, through their decisions, will shape the organization's future. Because workers are going to become more self-managing, workforce planning includes the integration of employees' goals as well as their talents and capabilities with organizational goals.

The most sought-after members of the strategic workforce will be able to:

- Figure out new ways to do things—to drop the baggage of the past and go on to something better
- Adjust to new structures and relationships rapidly while maintaining old alliances and networks
- Manage and work with diversity
- Perform technical skills competently
- Translate vision into day-to-day actions and decisions

This description may apply to certain previous employees who were laid off through no fault or deficiency of their own. They may have gone off and learned new capabilities from new employers or developed entrepreneurial skills independently. They may want to work full-time, part-time, or in a consulting capacity to contribute exactly the kinds of expertise the organization requires. If the organization has handled previous downsizings intelligently, fairly, and compassionately, they may be ready to join up again.

Both old and new members of the strategic workforce will be seeking careers in which they can apply their strongest skills and develop new ones. They will thrive best in an environment where their initiative is encouraged, their contributions are rewarded, and their career progress is unhampered by bureaucracy. In most organizations, current career paths do not meet these needs—especially for technical people, who reach the apex of their technical track early and then have nowhere to go but into management. Recognizing that attraction and retention of technological capability are critical, many organizations are developing dual career paths: one track for managers and another for people who may not have the desire or talent for management. Since there will be fewer and fewer managerial slots as organizations continue to go through resizing, it makes sense to ensure that the nonmanagement track is comparable to the management path in terms of competence, responsibility, influence, and rewards. With an emphasis on roles and skills rather than on "job boxes" and number of people supervised, the nonmanagerial career track also appeals to other types of independent contributors, such as engineers and legal experts.

The best time to initiate training and development programs for both core and contingent workers is immediately after a downsizing. (Of course, such programs need to be planned beforehand.) These offerings ought to include, in addition to training and education classes:

- Cross-training on the job
- Temporary assignments or internships in another company location, with another organization, in a university, or in the community
- Career assessment and planning workshops
- Rotating team assignments
- Task force leadership (e.g., chairing the United Way campaign or the work and family committee)

- Mentoring
- Special projects

Action-oriented development programs such as these present excellent opportunities to move employees out of postdownsizing paralysis and to begin integrating core and contingent staffs.

CONCLUSION

Downsizing affects not only those who lose their jobs, but also the organization as a whole system. Employers need to work on the following:

- Dealing with the emotions and behavior of those who remain
- Rethinking, together with employees, the way work should be done
- Planning for the needs of a new strategic workforce that provides essential skills for the future
- Encouraging employees to become self-managing
- Determining how to keep the organization flexible so that future downsizings can be minimal, manageable transitions

The goal of downsizing is not simply to become smaller, but to improve performance and, concurrently, the bottom line. This can happen only when the strong feelings engendered by downsizing are channeled into productive, creative action linked to a sense of purpose. Since the new workplace will not be the same as the old one, the organization cannot realize its potential if old behaviors preclude the introduction and implementation of new ideas.

12

The Revitalized Organization

Stuart Aubret was sitting in the Streeter-Haaz conference room, immersed in thought. It was the lunch hour, and the room had just emptied after an extremely productive planning meeting. The core issue was what to do about the steady decline in orders for the XK-11, a product based on aging technology that was still being manufactured.

Stuart thought back to a similar meeting two years earlier when the company had been faced with the decline in the SK and MK product lines. That meeting had launched one of the most troublesome periods in Streeter-Haaz's history. Managers had had to make difficult decisions about which valued employees to terminate, how to handle the survivors, and how to forge survivors and new hires into a successful new strategic workforce team. Because the company had been new to the downsizing process, morale had plummeted, and confusion, indecision, and uncertainty had lasted for weeks.

But today's meeting had been much different. Alicia Feingold, CFO, had presented the cost figures on the XK-11 and had projected that the product would begin losing money in about six weeks. Since it would then start draining cash away from the core business, her recommendation was to stop production of the XK-11. Executive VP Carlos Sanderson, who headed the strategic product planning task force, had agreed and had then turned the meeting over to SVP of Human Resources, Christina Perugia.

Christina had taken a minute to summarize the current workforce, pointing out that it would be relatively simple to reduce the temporary workforce by one hundred (a phone call to the temporary agency that had placed them) and not to renew the upcoming contracts for fifteen contract quality assurance engineers. Many of the staff engineers could be moved to other divisions, but about thirty remaining employees would probably have to seek employment outside Streeter-Haaz. However, she had assured the group, systems were in place to handle the downsizing smoothly, and the transition team was ready to swing into action. Their job would be easier this time around. Both employees and managers were better informed and better prepared to handle downsizing as they would any other business transition.

Nevertheless, Stuart was not satisfied to do the same things in the same way this time. What had Streeter-Haaz learned from the last downsizing? How could the process be improved? What goals were different now? Since technology and market forces were continually changing Streeter-Haaz's business parameters, the downsizing was not the company's last. He realized that resizing planning, which was integral to the reinvention of the business, needed to be built into his overall corporate strategy if the organization was to endure.

RENEWAL: RECOVERY OR TRANSFORMATION?

Because downsizing affects, and is affected by, virtually all the other systems and decisions in an organization, management cannot just dust off its hands and say, "Well, the organization is the size we want it now—thank goodness that's over with." Reductions in force may be necessary, but they are never sufficient. Planning is required before, during, and after a downsizing, as the company prepares to face future challenges. Postdownsizing planning is also predownsizing: rehearsing for the next wave.

As noted in chapter 1, downsizing can be an opportunity to strengthen the existing organization or to create a new corporate culture—or possibly to do both. It is appropriate for a postdownsized organization to take another look at the differences between a linear change and a total shift in the way the company thinks about itself. Figure 1 in chapter 1 can help managers and work teams assess what needs to be done and what that means in terms of the following:

- Which employees should be retained, retrained, or let go?
- Which systems should be changed?
- What types of behavior need to be rewarded?

A paradigm shift means wholesale transformation—a new set of guiding assumptions, behaviors, and definitions of success. Although recent management literature has implied that paradigm shift is the way to go, some organizations may not be quite ready for it. On the other hand, some are ready, or ought to be, but have not been paying enough attention to market indicators and are in danger of mortgaging their future by failing to make substantial, fundamental changes in a timely manner. Even if the immediate goal after downsizing is only to strengthen, not to transform, the organization needs to approach renewal with a clear notion of what it wants to be and an openness to new ideas. Otherwise it cannot be an enduring and successful competitor.

After a downsizing, the temptation is to resist change—to hold still and just breathe quietly after all the turbulence. However, this is the ideal time to reshape the organizational infrastructure and introduce processes that will further the achievement of business goals. The leaner structure is more flexible, and the employees are ready to focus on the future.

HOW WELL DID WE DO?

Before integrating restructuring strategies into long-term plans, management needs to assess what went right and what went wrong this time. A variety of studies of downsized organizations reveal that most of the cuts, to management's dismay, did not achieve the desired and expected goals. Costs were higher than anticipated, and payoffs were lower. These companies were chagrined to learn that staff reduction in itself is not enough to ensure an invigorated, more competitive organization.

In order to create an upward spiral of success, it is important to measure both the quantitative (financial/productivity) and qualitative (ability/attitude) results of each effort. The following checklist is a guideline for evaluation. The questionnaire should be tailored to the performance results the organization expects to achieve through downsizing.

Checklist for Evaluation

❑ Environment
  - What has the downsizing achieved for our customers?
  - Is our competitive position better now?
  - How do those outside the organization—the public, the media, vendors, customers, and the labor pool from which new employees will be drawn—view it today?

❑ Structure
  - Have we reduced the levels of decision making? Are our decisions significantly more timely?
  - Have we cascaded responsibilities down to lower levels?
  - Is the "bureaucratic bloat" history?

❑ Technology
  - How have we changed our processes to reduce costs and time and add value for our customers?
  - Does our workforce match our technical strategy?

❑ Tasks
  - Have we reinvented tasks to accomplish the desired work of the organization?
  - To what extent have quality and volume of output increased or decreased?

❑ People
  - Do the remaining employees have the skills required to perform the key tasks required for the business to succeed?
  - To what extent has the motivation level among the surviving employees increased or decreased?
  - How do these employees view the organization?

❑ General
  - To what extent have expenses been reduced, or increased, in the period since the downsizing?
  - To what extent are profits projected to increase or diminish?
  - To what extent has the shareholders' return on investment increased or diminished?
  - What particular aspects of the downsizing were favorably or unfavorably viewed by the company's various stakeholders?

- Quality of communications to employees
- Selection and effectiveness of downsizing options used
- Length of notice given to those whose jobs were affected
- Quality of outplacement and assistance programs

Some of these questions—for example, those involving structure and image—can be asked as early as two weeks after the downsizing. Others can be asked within two months and repeatedly thereafter. The answers will provide the benchmarks for measuring the success of future resizing programs. Additional benchmarks can be specified by comparing results with those of similar organizations' downsizing efforts.

Admittedly, acquiring the data may prove difficult; most organizations have not established Total Quality programs for downsizing. Often, in fact, they shy away from measuring an activity they would rather not have performed in the first place. However, evaluation, in measures as specific as possible, provides not only a benchmark but also an indication of what should be done differently in the future. As organizations become more comfortable with the concept of restructuring as a normal, recurrent, manageable transition, measures will become more standardized. In the meantime, information can be gleaned from a variety of sources:

- Standard financial analyses and productivity measures; since these effects usually cannot all be attributed to the downsizing itself, a comparison with projected downsizing results will be necessary
- Surveys of affected groups
- Internal communication and feedback systems
- Analysis of media reports

For a comparison with other companies in the industry, management can turn to studies by career transition and consulting firms and to its own board of directors, which should contain a diversity of experience and knowledge. The board can also add to the data from shareholders and perhaps other stakeholders, particularly customers, as well.

In a global organization, effects of restructuring will probably vary from one location to another. In assessing the relative impact of each, management needs to determine whether too much attention was paid to corporate headquarters and too little to the field. Assessment measures will have to be tailored to the diversity of cultures involved as well as to the local regulations and business practices.

The downsized organization typically finds itself with a streamlined structure and a sharper focus on the core business. With fewer layers of management, decision making can be pushed down to lower levels and can be more flexible and responsive to stakeholder needs. Now, the organization is in a better position to empower and strengthen its strategic workforce. Because empowerment is the antithesis of patriarchy, the renewed organization will operate most effectively with the following mindset:

> The renewed organization will be successful only if it views its employees as partners in the change process: as consenting, even initiating, adults rather than children who follow rules established by others. If employees help create change, they will be less resistant to it. And the business will gain, often in surprising ways, from their active participation and insights.

Areas in which employees have been successfully involved in the organizational change process include the following:

Creating the organizational vision. Increasingly, managers and employees together are creating vision statements indicating what the organization aims to be—different from a mission statement that says what it intends to do—and developing workable management philosophies that spell out what kinds of behavior are necessary to realize the vision. In today's workplace, management is everybody's business.

Planning and managing operations. Self-managing work teams are (a) planning work flow, (b) making hiring, firing, and work load decisions and, in the process, (c) learning how to work together smoothly with a shared sense of purpose.

Total Quality programs. Employees, who are close to the customer, are applying the vision to the question, How much of what we do is based on our own structure, and how much is based on value to our customers? For example, a particular packaging process might fit the company's current assembly line procedures, but a Total Quality team might learn that the customer thinks the packaging is cumbersome for unpacking and shelf stocking.

Job redesign. In several companies, including National Semiconductor and British Petroleum, teams of employees from all levels and functions have created dual career paths, specifying the key tasks required for each step up each path. General Electric, which eliminated more than 100,000 jobs in a series of downsizings, gathers groups of employees for three-day forums to determine how to take unnecessary work out of their jobs and solve problems together.

Technology planning.   Organizations are discovering that technical expertise—essential in today's information-based business climate—is more likely to be found in the trenches than in the boardroom. They are tapping that expertise, sometimes through interactive media provided by technology itself—for example, information and communication systems linking employees around the globe.

INTEGRATING RESIZING INTO BUSINESS STRATEGY

Even if the organization has done everything "right" in downsizing, the process will no doubt have to be repeated since marketplace conditions are so fluid. These conditions will probably be different the next time around. The five critical business elements—business environment, structure, technology, tasks, and people—will have undergone further changes. All these elements play central roles in strategic planning and its subsystem, workforce planning.

Because workforce planning affects every other aspect of strategic planning, line executives cannot hand the restructuring portion off to the human resources department and forget about it. The human resources department is the one best suited to overseeing many aspects of downsizing, such as ensuring accuracy of benefits and pay statements, designing training programs, and facilitating job and role reassignments, but it cannot operate outside a strategic business context.

SVP Elizabeth Lamond, in charge of long-range strategic planning, sat across the conference room table from Human Resources' Christina Perugia, Legal's Elaine Steinhauer, and Corporate Communications' Nathan Gottleib. At her side was senior vice president Ashley Sarasua, head of the engineering department. Elizabeth has convened the meeting to impart some important news: Ashley has been named program manager for downsizing and transition, a role in which she was to pull together information and resources from various departments in the company: legal, corporate communications, human resources, and line operations. Her responsibilities, both strategic and tactical, would span the predownsizing (before), downsizing (during), and postdownsizing (after) phases. They included the following:

Before

- Working with line departments to determine which tasks were essential for the present and the future and which would be changing
- Facilitating meetings to select options for downsizing
- Heading the transition team

During

- Working with line managers to ensure that all downsizing activities were on schedule and that communications were timely and appropriate
- Assisting in coordinating internal and external resources

After

- Assisting line management in coordinating evaluation programs
- Working with human resources to ensure that recognition and reward programs were consistent with the company's new ways of doing business
- Researching the best downsizing practices of other organizations within and outside the industry
- Participating in corporate long-range planning meetings

Since many of these activities previously fell under the purview of Elizabeth, it was clear that Ashley was being groomed for higher positions in the company. The program manager assignment, which would not be full-time, was nevertheless substantial enough that some of Ashley's work in the engineering department was being reassigned to her second-in-command, Tony Jackson. He, in turn, would gain experience enabling him to enhance his own career.

Strategic planning of workforce size, drawing on the knowledge of line as well as staff people, should focus on the skills—as opposed to the positions—needed for the future. Of course, the future is largely unknowable. Therefore, flexibility must be built into the planning process. Planners need to update themselves continually regarding certain basic questions:

- What skills do we need?
- Which essential skills are available in the labor pool from which we hire?
- How can we attract the kinds of people we seek?
- What do these people desire from work and from their employer?
- Which skills are in short supply? What kinds of training and retraining will we need to do? What skill needs should be filled by people and organizations outside our own firm?
- How can we capitalize on the talents of a diverse workforce?
- Are we keeping employees informed about business conditions and their roles in the organization? How can we involve them in decision making?
- How can we tailor outplacement and counseling services, in-house and contracted, to our particular requirements?
- What is our policy regarding reductions in force?

POLICY

This last subject requires some elaboration. The first time an organization undergoes resizing, policies may shift from month to month and sometimes from unit to unit. For example, the overall policy may begin with "no layoffs" and move through "voluntary moves only" to "meet higher performance standards" to "layoffs." Outplacement procedures and degree of advance notice given may also vary from one situation to another. No wonder employees are confused, paralyzed, and suspicious. Both employees and management need clear parameters so that they can plan their own work and move ahead with confidence. The organization should not make commitments (e.g., "no layoffs") that it may not be able to keep. The policy should, however, specify the order in which the various downsizing options will be pursued and the order in which different segments of the workforce—for example, contract, temporary, part-time, permanent—will be affected.

CONCLUSION

Planning the size and shape of the workforce is integral to an organization's long-term strategic planning and critical enough to warrant continuous attention, resources, and strong, enlightened leadership.

Restructuring should be regarded as one alternative, but not necessarily the last alternative. As part of the entire revisioning and resizing process, it requires repeated measurement and readjustment to achieve desired results. Because the need for resizing will be a constant force, planning before and after resizing efforts are related tasks. And because the vitality of the organization depends on how well these tasks dovetail with long-range strategic goals, certain basic questions demand constant attention as the organization evolves:

- In view of interrelated developments, current and projected, internal and external, what will our skill needs be?
- Does the organization need to be reinvented or just restored, or both? How will each type of change affect our workforce?
- What, specifically, can we achieve by resizing? What results do we expect?

Employees, whose careers depend on the answers to these questions as well as on their own motivations and efforts, must be part of the planning process. It is important to bring them, as well as other stakeholders, into the process early, not only to minimize the negative effects of downsizing but also to reap the benefits of these stakeholders' knowledge, their insights, and the synergy between the top-down view and the bottom-up and sideways view.

With an integrated strategy, collaborative planning, and effective communication, downsizing becomes a manageable and measurable transition. Instead of badly handling a restructuring, organizations need to embrace its challenges and capitalize on its inherent opportunities.

References

Gordon, Jack (Ed.). 1991. Seventh annual training zone awards. *Training Magazine*, December, p. 42.

Gyr, Herman. 1991. *Enterprise development: Organizational diagnosis.* Palo Alto, CA: Co-Development Associates.

Handy, Charles. 1990. *The age of unreason.* Boston: Harvard Business School Press.

Kennedy Publications. 1990. *An analysis of the outplacement consulting business in North America* (p. 12). Fitzwilliam, NH: Kennedy Publications.

OITC Tax Bulletin. August 21, 1992. p. 1. (For information contact Association of Outplacement Consulting Firms International, 1101 Connecticut Avenue, NW, Suite 700, Washington, DC 20036.)

Right Associates. 1990. *Severance: The corporate response.* Philadelphia: Right Asssociates.

———. 1992. *Lessons learned.* Philadelphia: Right Asssociates.

Wendelton, Kate. 1992. *Through the brick wall: How to job hunt in a tight market.* New York: Villard Books.

The Wyatt Company. 1993. *Best practices in corporate restructuring.* Washington, DC: The Wyatt Company.

Index

235